In the Storm
His Love

A Ménière's & Vestibular Project
of *Faith*, *Love* and *Hope*

In the Storm *His Love*
© 2025 Lilly Pilly *Grace* Publishing
Julieann Wallace, Heather Davies, Angela Selar, Steve Schwier,
Dave Giugno, G. Lakin Rosier, and Kim M. Rosier

No AI has been used in the creation of this book.

A collection of prayer, poems, songs, faith stories and art, praising, thanking and honoring our beautiful God, from people living with Ménière's disease and vestibular conditions including vestibular migraine, collated by Julieann Wallace, in collaboration with Heather Davies, G Lakin Rosier II, Angela Selar, Dave Giugno, and Steven Schwier. *Profits from this book will be donated to medical research to help find successful treatments.*

All rights reserved.

No part of this publication may be reproduced, stored in a retrieval system or transmitted, in any form or by any means, electronic, mechanical, photocopying, recording or otherwise, without prior written permission of the copyright holder, including for training of the hallucinating AI.

'Scriptures and additional materials quoted are from the Good News Bible © 1994 published by the British and Foreign Bible Society. Good News Bible © American Bible Society 1966, 1971, 1976, 1992. Used with permission.'

ISBN: 978-1-7643118-8-5 print book
    978-1-7643118-7-8 eBook
Cover design by Lilly Pilly Publishing
Cover image by Adobe Stock
Interior images Creative Market

Artwork by artists retain copyright of their work.
Writings from people retain copyright of their work.

All errors in the book are ours.

2 Corinthians 1:3-4

Praise be to the God and Father
of our Lord Jesus Christ,
the Father of compassion and the God of all comfort,
who comforts us in all our troubles, so that we can
comfort those in any trouble with the comfort we
ourselves receive from God.

Psalm 150:6

Let everything that has breath praise the Lord.

Contents

About i

Poetry and Songs 1

Scripture 13

Stories of Faith 49

Art 125

Prayer .181

Acknowledgements 219

Behind the Book 221

About

Ménière's disease is a chronic inner ear disorder causing:
- unpredictable, disabling episodes of vertigo (spinning)
- fluctuating hearing loss, deafness, tinnitus (ringing in the ear)
- and a feeling of ear fullness

These episodes (attacks) can last for anywhere from twenty minutes to several hours. As if the symptoms above weren't enough, they can be accompanied by nausea, lingering fatigue, and imbalance which can last for several days.

Researchers believe Ménière's is caused by genetics, inflammatory response (to head trauma, viruses, bacterial infections, auto-immune inner ear disease, systemic inflammation) or is noise-induced. (*Professor Jose Antonio Lopez Escamez,* et al). It is now believed that Ménière's is not a *single* condition - the symptoms may all be similar but the causes are varied, and identifiable. Up to 40% of patients may have a *genetic origin* for their Ménière's, whilst the other 60% have some kind of *immune system* problem. Amongst the immune subgroup, there are 3 additional distinct categories, all identifiable via blood tests - *auto-immune, allergic inflammation or auto-inflammation.* These discoveries will lead to individualised and successful treatments.

Vestibular Migraine is a neurological disorder where migraine affects part of the brain that controls balance. Along with the "typical" migraine symptoms like sound and light sensitivity, visual aura, nausea and vomiting, brain fog, headache and pressure in ears, people with vestibular migraine may experience any combination of these symptoms:
- Vertigo
- Dizziness
- Unsteadiness and loss of balance
- Sensitivity to motion and visual stimuli
- Migraine - with or without headache pain
- Numbness and tingling down one side of the head/face

These episodes (attacks) can last minutes to hours and are often said to be brought on by stress, nutritional triggers, lack of sleep, weather, dehydration or hormonal changes.

Both of these invisible vestibular disorders deeply affect nearly every aspect of an individual's life, physically, mentally, socially, financially and spiritually.

Poetry and Song

Ephesians 5:19

*Speak to one another with psalms, hymns,
and songs from the Spirit.
Sing and make music from
your heart to the Lord.*

The Space Between

Michelle Kelly

The space between
The responsibility
The expectations
The labels
The rules
The judgement
The fear
There is a space between all this heaviness.
A space that feels *safe, light, free* and *open*.
This space allows for
Connection
Presence
Authenticity
Purpose
Peace
Joy
Beauty
Love
This space is within you, God, always!

Diagnosed with vestibular migraine

Where Were You?

Heather Davies

Where were You when I began to lose myself?
Where were You when I no longer
recognized the person in the mirror?
Where were You when my tears fell quietly in the shower?
Where were You when the doctor said, "It's all in your head"
and I began to wonder if he was right?
Where were You when the silence from
friends became deafening?
Where were You when the weight of being
a burden to my husband weighed heavily on my heart?
Where were You when I grew sicker than
the patients I cared for?

Where were You?

Looking back today, I see You.
I see You there, when I began to lose myself
to negative thoughts,
You weaved positive ones amongst the darkest.
I see You now in the quiet of the shower,
Your strength washing over me.
I see You in one of doctors placed along my path,
honest enough to say, "I don't know,
but we will find the answers together".
I see You in the silence of severed friendships,
leading me to strangers who showed me
how to love myself again.
I see You in the weight of my burdens,
lifting me when I choose calm over chaos,
and gratitude over fear.

You were there.

You were in the stillness, in my deep breaths,
in the peace that washed over my panic.
You were there through it all,
I just needed to open my heart to see You.

You were there.

From Silence, I Soar Like a Butterfly

Jenny Chaves

I was once a young caterpillar, small and free,
Crawling through life carefree with joy and glee.
The world sang softly, laughter and light,
Every sound a treasure, every day bright.

Then silence came, a cocoon tight and still,
Wrapping around me against my will.
Ménière's disease stole the music I knew,
Robbing my hearing ability too.

Nausea, fear, and vertigo spins in the night,
Isolation pressing with heavy might.
Independence faltered, confidence shook,
I feared I'd never again embrace the world I once took.

I thought my life would never be the same,
That darkness had won, and I was to blame.
But faith whispered softly, a gentle thread,
"Rise again, through the path which you are lead."

I found my courage in quiet ways,
Seeking help and light through the haze.
Doctors, care, treatments sought and tried,
Strength returning as I fought desperately inside.

Fear of surgery loomed like a towering wall,
Heart racing, doubt threatening to stall.
But love called louder—my daughter's voice,
A melody of hope, a reason to rejoice.

I broke the cocoon, wings trembling, bright,
Burst into the world, embracing the light.
Though hearing is changed, though health is not whole,
I rise anew, body and soul.

I fly in wind, I feel, I see,
The world around still speaking to me.
Though life is altered, and scars remain,
Faith and courage turned struggle to gain.

The caterpillar is gone; the butterfly thrives,
Stronger, wiser, different - embracing my new life.
From silence, from pain, from fear and strife,
I have emerged… what a beautiful life!

Every whisper of wind, every ray of sun,
Every laugh, every voice, every day begun,
Reminds me of the journey, the battles won,
Of faith and strength, and the rising I've done.

From silence, I soar, with wings of grace,
Facing the world with courage in place.
Though hearing is different, though challenges stay,
I still live, I still love, I rise every day.

His Grace is enough

Sailing For The Lord
A song

Lisa K. Champion, 1995

Verse 1

Sailing On the water
Sailing toward the sun
Sailing toward the future
Whatever comes along
We're sailing for eternal life
And we're sailing for the Lord

Chorus:

Let the sail up
Let the winds blow
God is your guide
His path He'll show
Let your light shine
Let your praises flow
Let your praises flow

Verse 2

Some days will be hard
Rapids and storms
But we must look ahead
For the gift that will come
We're sailing for eternal life
And we're sailing for the Lord

(Chorus)

Verse 3

When things go wrong
Learn to sail on
Take one day at a time
Forgiveness is yours and mine
We're sailing for eternal life
And we're sailing for the Lord

(Chorus)

Scripture

2 Timothy 3:16–17

All scripture is breathed out by God and profitable for teaching, for reproof, for correction, and for training in righteousness, that the man of God may be complete, equipped for every good work.

Romans 15:4

For whatever was written in former days was written for our instruction, that through endurance and through the encouragement of the scriptures we might have hope.

Exodus 14:14

The Lord will fight for you;
you need only to be still.

Isaiah 29:18

And in that day shall the deaf hear the words of the book, and the eyes of the blind shall see out of obscurity, and out of darkness.

Philippians 4:19

And my God will meet all your needs
according to the riches of His glory in Christ Jesus.

Isaiah 35:5

Then the eyes of the blind shall be opened,
and the ears of the deaf shall be unstopped.

James 1:12

Blessed is the one who perseveres under trial because,
having stood the test, that person will receive
the crown of life that the Lord has promised
to those who love him.

2 Corinthians 5:7

For we walk by faith,
not by sight.

Jeremiah 30:17

'But I will restore you to health and heal your wounds,' declares the LORD.

Psalm 9:1

I will give thanks to You, Lord, with all my heart;
I will tell of all Your wonderful deeds.

Revelations 21:4

He will wipe every tear from their eyes.
There will be no more death
or mourning or crying or pain,
for the old order of things has passed away.

Isaiah 33:2

Lord, be gracious to us; we long for You.
Be our strength every morning,
our salvation in time of distress.

Matthew 11:28–30

Come to me, all you who are weary and burdened,
and I will give you rest.
Take my yoke upon you and learn from me,
for I am gentle and humble in heart,
and you will find rest for your souls.
For My yoke is easy and My burden is light.

Isaiah 40:29

He gives strength to the weary
and increases the power of the weak.

Psalm 147:3

He heals the brokenhearted
and binds up their wounds.

Psalm 23

The Lord is my shepherd, I lack nothing.
He makes me lie down in green pastures,
He leads me beside quiet waters, He refreshes my soul.
He guides me along the right paths for His name's sake.
Even though I walk through the darkest valley,
I will fear no evil, for You are with me;
Your rod and Your staff, they comfort me.
You prepare a table before me
in the presence of my enemies.
You anoint my head with oil; my cup overflows.
Surely Your goodness and love will follow me
all the days of my life,
and I will dwell in the house of the Lord forever.

John 3:16

For God so loved the world
that He gave his one and only Son,
that whoever believes in Him shall not perish
but have eternal life.

2 Corinthians 1:3-4

Praise be to the God
and Father of our Lord Jesus Christ,
the Father of compassion and the God of all comfort,
who comforts us in all our troubles,
so that we can comfort those in any trouble
with the comfort we ourselves receive from God.

Isaiah 25:1

Lord, You are my God;
I will exalt You and praise Your name,
for in perfect faithfulness You have done
wonderful things,
things planned long ago.

Psalm 28:7

The Lord is my strength and my shield;
my heart trusts in Him, and He helps me.
My heart leaps for joy,
and with my song I praise him.

Psalm 145:1

I will exalt You,
my God the King;
I will praise Your name
for ever and ever.

Psalm 150:6

Let everything that has breath praise the Lord.

Philippians 4:13

I can do all this through Him
who gives me strength.

Psalm 68:19

Praise be to the Lord,
to God our Savior,
who daily bears our burdens.

Deuteronomy 31:6

Be strong and courageous.
Do not fear or be in dread of them,
for it is the Lord your God who goes with you.
He will not leave you or forsake you.

Philippians 4:6–7

Do not be anxious about anything,
but in every situation, by prayer and petition,
with thanksgiving, present your requests to God.
And the peace of God,
which transcends all understanding,
will guard your hearts and your minds in Christ Jesus.

Psalm 42:5

Why are you cast down, O my soul,
and why are you in turmoil within me?
Hope in God;
for I shall again praise Him, my salvation.

Psalm 46:10

Be still,
and know that I am God.

Psalm 69:30

I will praise the name of God with a song;
I will magnify Him with thanksgiving.

Isaiah 43:2

When you pass through the waters,
I will be with you;
and through the rivers, they shall not overwhelm you;
when you walk through fire
you shall not be burned,
and the flame shall not consume you.

Jeremiah 17:14

Heal me, O Lord, and I shall be healed;
save me, and I shall be saved,
for You are my praise.

2 Corinthians 12:9–10

My grace is sufficient for you,
for my power is made perfect in weakness.
Therefore I will boast all the more gladly
of my weaknesses, so that the
power of Christ may rest upon me.
For the sake of Christ, then,
I am content with weaknesses, insults, hardships,
persecutions, and calamities.
For when I am weak, then I am strong.

1 Thessalonians 5:16-18

Rejoice always,
pray continually,
give thanks in all circumstances;
for this is God's will for you in Christ Jesus.

Deuteronomy 31:8

The Lord himself goes before you
and will be with you;
He will never leave you nor forsake you.
Do not be afraid;
do not be discouraged.

When peace like a river, attendeth my way,
when sorrows like sea billows roll;
whatever my lot, Thou hast taught me to say,
"It is well, it is well with my soul."

Horatio G. Spafford, 1873

Consider this...
(not scripture, but something to think about)

Paul had difficulty with his eyesight
that God never healed.
Paul had a thorn in the flesh
which he prayed for God to remove
over and over again,
but God never removed it.

Job suffered because God had a much
bigger purpose for him than just
contentedness on the Earth.
Job's suffering was not due to the result
of a lack of faith.

God's got this!

Stories of Faith

Mark 5:19

Return to your home,
and declare how much God has done for you.

2 Corinthians 1:3-4

Blessed be the God and Father
of our Lord Jesus Christ,
the Father of mercies and God of all comfort,
who comforts us in all our affliction, so that we may
be able to comfort those who are in any affliction,
with the comfort with which we ourselves are
comforted by God.

The Day of the Lily

Heather Davies

The calm that washed over me that day was unlike anything I'd ever felt. My mother and I walked hand in hand through the sterile, all-white corridor of the freshly painted Emergency Room. It felt as though our feet never touched the floor. As gravity tenderly released its anchor, we floated quietly, peacefully through the halls.

No words were spoken, a simple squeeze of her hand said everything my heart needed. A calm so deep it silenced my fear.

As the hospital doors parted, we walked through. The warmth of the sun gently caressed my face, allowing me to finally exhale, shedding the weight of the diagnosis we had been given: a brain tumor.

My eyes caught sight of a small parking lot planter, filled with sun-bleached mulch and a single white lily, its center brushed with purple and yellow hues. One lone bloom, so out of place, yet... perfectly placed. It seemed to whisper, *Give it all to Me*.

I paused, lifted my phone and captured the moment. That day, I began the practice of pausing, of noticing beauty even when the world tilts, spins and seems so ugly and painful. I have paused many times since, trusting those moments of awe to carry me.

On the day of the lily, I was given a diagnosis that shook me to my core, but it also awakened something deep within me. It stripped away the noise of my busy life and left only what was real, the beauty that heals, the stillness that reminds me He carries us through.

Darkness and light.
Sickness and health.
Hard and easy.
Hurting and healing.
Loss and love.
All of it can coexist because His love threads through it all.

I remember that feeling, the weight lifting from my shoulders, cleansing my entire soul of the ache deep within, of a diagnosis I never saw coming. His unseen hands had taken it from me, while walking through that corridor.

He held me.
He held me then, He holds me still.
His love is so palpable it takes my breath away.

Faith
Love
Hope

Your Faith Has Made You Whole
(Matthew 9:22, Mark 5:34, Luke 18:42)

G Lakin Rosier II

I have had people tell me, "I have not been healed because I do not have enough faith. After all, Jesus said that if you have faith the size of a mustard seed, you can move mountains." *(Matthew 17:20)*.

Others have also quoted Jesus, "Ask and you shall receive!" *(Matthew 7:7-8)*. However, they ignore *1 John 5:14* that states:

> "And this is the confidence that we have in him, that, if we ask any thing according to his will, he heareth us."

According to his will is a key phase. God can see the *eternal* perspective, while we only have a limited view from our mortal perspective.

I once taught a youth Sunday school lesson where I blind folded one of the students and hung a tapestry on the wall. I had the student stand with his toes against the wall and press his nose to the tapestry. I removed the blind fold and asked him, what was depicted on the tapestry. All he could tell me was it was brown.

The rest of the class knew it was a running horse.

Like that student, our mortal view point only allows us to see the brown. God not only sees the horse, He sees the classroom, the rest of the earth, all of the cosmos, and all of that through all eternity.

Jesus said, "You were made whole by your faith." *(Mark 5:34 & Luke 17:19).*

When I was told I was not healed because I lacked faith, I felt depressed, and even upset with God. I felt I had faith *at least* the size of a mustard seed.

Over the years, I spoke with various people on the subject, listened to lessons taught in Sunday school, and talks given by church leaders. They taught me that overcoming a mountain is a metaphor for overcoming an insurmountable object. Moving a mountain was an impossible task when Jesus walked the earth.

When Jesus told the woman with the issue of blood, and the blind man, that they were made whole, he was not just referring to their physical ailments. He was stating they were whole *in Christ by their faith.*

The healing will come at God's time, which might not even be in this lifetime. We are told that in the afterlife that not a hair on your head shall be lost, and our body will be made perfect. To be made whole in Christ means to be made spiritually whole.

Jesus is capable of healing each of us, but with his eternal perspective, He may see that is not what would be best for us. Jesus healed the ten lepers, but only one praised God and thanked Him. The other nine were physically healed, but not made whole in Christ. Only the one leper who praised God and thanked Jesus was made whole in Christ.

All of us have overcome mountains in our lives. We have done, and will continue to do, things we once would have thought impossible. We have dealt with things we never thought we would be able to deal with. We should be like the one leper, *praise God* and *thank Jesus* for those times.

Even the small things.

Some days, doing tasks a person without a chronic illness would think nothing about doing, seems to be as impossible as moving a mountain. Just doing a load of laundry can seem impossible to us at times, but we have clean clothes to wear, at least *most* days we do.

My belief in Christ has changed who I am as a person, and for the better. I was diagnosed with Ménière's around 2010, but my current doctor thinks my first symptoms started around 1980, in my teenage years.

Maybe even childhood.

I did not grow up in a religious home, and did not believe in any religion. I was not even sure there was a God. I had a minor curiosity in what people believed, but more often teased them for their beliefs.

Over the years I had many discussions about religion with people of various faiths, including many different Christian denominations, but none of them made sense to me.

My first step came one day when I saw a poster with the poem *Footprints on the Sand* by Mary Stevenson. The last verse hit me hard, *The Lord replied, "The times when you have seen only one set of footprints, my child, is when I carried you."*

When I was nearly forty years old, I learned about Jesus because, while planning to get married to Kim Rosier, she wanted me to learn about her beliefs so I could understand her better.

She stated she would not push me to believe what she believed, or to join the church. She just wanted me to understand her better.

That made sense to me. It was not until a couple years after the wedding that I was taught about what she believed in. It was the first time I understood, and I believed what I was told, and I could not deny the truth. I soon joined the church and started attending regularly for the first time in my life.

In my 20s and 30s I was a jerk, to put it mildly. I worked as a cook in restaurants and was known to make waitresses cry by the way I treated them. I treated everyone poorly. In biblical terms, you could say I had the spirit of contention about me.

When I learned of Christ, and the need to be more like him, I worked hard to become a better person. I'm still working on growing my faith, learning what it means to be like Christ, and trying to be whole in Christ.

In the meantime, Jesus helps me to move my mountains, which in return helps grow my faith.

Hallelujah

Overcoming

Julieann Wallace

When I was eight-years-old, I heard the voice of God. Me. An unassuming, energetic, zippy little girl was stilled for a moment in time at the sound of *His* voice. Little did I know at the time, how much I would lean on God to get me through the storms in my life. I want to cry as I look back. I'm overwhelmed by His love, His mercy, His grace, His pursuit. His polishing of my faith so that I love Him with all my heart, all of my mind, all of my strength and all of my soul.

He is more beautiful than you can ever imagine!

On October 31st, and November 1st, 2025, *Cochlear Australia* invited me to Sydney, Australia, for a photoshoot and filming about my cochlear implant, and the *Cochlear Buddy Program* I am involved in. Ménière's disease took my hearing. Devastating. Heartbreaking. In my interviews I had two things I absolutely wanted recorded on film - Ménière's disease, for awareness and to honour my fellow Ménièrians, and my answered prayer of returned hearing, to honour God. Mission accomplished!

My husband had my iPhone while I was being filmed in the studio, and saw notifications rolling in from people wanting to talk to me about Ménière's or cochlear implants. He told the group sitting around (Cochlear Australia employees and other Cochlear Implant Buddies) as they sat in a circle waiting for the next person to go in for filming. My husband said they were astounded. He told them that Ménière's was the monster in my life, and because it was so life changing for me, that I liked to help others through it.

When he told me this afterward, I sucked in a sharp breath. How right he was. I hadn't looked at Ménière's from that perspective.

Ménière's *was* a monster in my life.

A giant.

I had called it the Ménière's monster in Ménière's groups many times in my life over the thirty-one years that I had it. I was the one who originally used *Ménière's Warrior* in about 2013, now used around the world. But when my husband called it a "monster", it meant something different. It meant something far more serious and vicious.

There's a song we sing in church called 'Giants' (Citipointe Music). When it was first released the words hit deeply. It brought tears to my eyes when I first sang it, and still does. Ménière's was one of my giants.

(from Giants, written by *Colin Moore* and *Beau Lamshed*)

Though I am afflicted, I'm not crushed
Though I am confused, I won't give up,
Though I've been cast down, I have not been broken
You're standing with me now, yeah
You're standing with me now, woah

So I will fear no evil, for You come to my defense
The victory was settled when You died and rose again
I will be strong and carry on, for You have gone before me
So I will fear no evil, for my God is able
Able, able
Woah
More than enough
You're more than enough, Lord

You're under my feet, oh giant
For the King has overcome
In the battle, You triumph
Our God, our Champion
You're under my feet, oh giant
For the King has overcome
In the battle, You triumph
Our God, our Champion
You're under my feet, oh giant
For the King has overcome
In the battle, You triumph
Our God, our Champion
You're under my feet, oh giant
For the King has overcome
In the battle, You triumph
Our God, our Champion

My husband often talks about how difficult it was to see me suffering with vertigo, and then the hearing loss and the tinnitus, watching the life being drained out of me. He felt hopeless. There was nothing he could do for me as a bystander.

It wasn't until I was *through the storm*, by the grace of God, that I could see from his perspective. My throat tightens when I think of how my Ménière's made him feel. It doesn't just affect the person with Ménière's, it affects those around them.

During one particularly violent and long vertigo attack, my mum was on her knees beside my bed, praying to God to take it away from me and to give it to her. I yelled NO! because you would never wish this disease on anyone.

At the time of my worst Ménière's symptoms, I was struggling to keep hanging on to life, my hand outstretched to God to help me. To save me. I was a mum to three young children. And I didn't want to be here anymore. I couldn't do the violent spinning vertigo that is akin to torture forty plus times a year. Three to four hours of staring at one spot on the wall, unable to move because it would make the vertigo impossibly worse. I would repeat the words over and over, 'I can't do this anymore! I can't do this anymore!' as I tried to control the nausea and vomiting with a breathing technique I self-learned. Necessity is a great teacher. It would only worked for a bit before the inevitable vomit-tron happened. All my husband could do was empty my vomit buckets and watch my tears fall while caring for our three young children.

I wanted an end to the torture of violent vertigo. It's something you would never wish on your worst enemy. While staring at that one spot on the wall, after I was finished with repeating the words 'I can't do this anymore!', I would picture myself in heaven, bowing down before God with the angels, singing and praising Him. *That* is what got me through. And the fact that one day, this torture would end.

I had a dream once, in the deep and dark days of struggling with my mental health on top of the Ménière's symptoms. I woke from that dream with hope. It was the year 2000.

In the dream I was sitting in a church (please note, I wasn't going to church at that time). And it was my cousin, *Darlene Zschech* and her husband, Mark's church (she did not have a church at that time – she does now). Darlene called me up to the stage. I froze in panic. In my dream, my breath quickened and I remember thinking in my panic, 'God will give you the words to speak'. And so, I made my way up on to the stage, and there I was, speaking to the congregation. These are the words that came to me:

'We live in the moment, and can't see beyond our struggles. But God sees us. Our life, from the beginning to the end. He sees your whole life, and what you are going through. This is where you are,' I said, spreading my hands apart to show about 20 centimetres (7 inches) in length, 'in this moment in time, compared to this.' I spread my hands as far apart as I could. 'It will get better.'

What a revelation!

You can read more details of my dream on page 103.

Falling

In 2004, God answered my prayer of stopping the vertigo. I decided to have gentamicin injected into my middle ear to destroy my balance cells and the signals from my inner ear to my brain that told me I was spinning, when in reality I wasn't. It also meant that I would have to relearn to walk again with a new balance. It also meant that I was choosing to destroy my hearing.

Imagine having to make that decision...

My reasoning was this: I can relearn to walk. I can still live a life with one good hearing ear, but I can't live a quality of life with the violent, unpredictable vertigo making me a prisoner in my own body. Taking everything from me.

When I talk about vertigo, I'm not just talking about being "dizzy". The vertigo of Ménière's disease for me, was the most abhorrent, violent, room spinning. Totally debilitating. It was "hold on to the floor or the bed even though you are already on lying on the floor or bed". I had to stare at one spot on the wall for three to four hours until the spinning subsided. And whatever you do, DON'T move your head. It will make the spinning one hundred times worse.

Beyond exhausting.

Soul destroying.

And let's not forget the relentless, vicious puking that feels like you're about to turn inside-out, dehydrating the body so much you need to be taken to hospital emergency.

If you ever want to know how vertigo of Ménière's feels, sit on an office swivel chair and get someone to spin you around and around and around as fast as they can.

Now, imagine not being able to stop it. Not being able to get off that office chair for hours and hours and hours. Then imagine, never being able to predict when vertigo will hit – and when it does, you are stuck wherever you are, and you absolutely cannot move, as it will make the spinning impossibly worse.

This is the vertigo of Ménière's. Hell.

How thankful to God I am that the gentamicin stopped my vertigo. I went back to teaching after three weeks.

Joy returned to my life. I no longer lived with fear of vertigo every moment of my life, sometimes waking me from my sleep.

But now I had a risk of falling. And I did.

Falling is never a good thing. And if you have your balance cells destroyed, when you fall, you have no idea where to place your hands to protect yourself.

The first time I fell was Christmas, 2018. My family and I were on holiday in Tasmania, Australia, walking the Dove Lake trek at Cradle Mountain. 5.7 km. 3 hours walking time.

I wrote about it my book, 'It Will Change Your Life – a cochlear implant journey'. Here's an excerpt:

> After the walk we entered the cafeteria for a drink. Without warning, tears filled my eyes. In public.
>
> My husband turned to me and the look on his face said it all. His eyes widened. 'What's wrong?'
>
> 'I fell,' I said. I wanted to sob. Loudly. Aftershock from the fall. I caught the sob in my throat. 'I fell and I couldn't stop it.'
>
> His eyes filled with tears, but they didn't leak down his cheek like mine. I always hate seeing his eyes that way. He was following me as we walked, to catch me if I fell. He always does that for me. My protector. And when it happened, there was no way he could stop it. I remember the panic in his voice as he leaned over me, asking if I was okay, looking over me, again and again. 'Did you hurt yourself?' he had asked.
>
> All I could say was, 'My phone is under the bush, over there.' I had no idea how I saw it slide under the bush. When I fall I have no idea where to put my hands to stop me, or protect me – inside my head as I'm falling, I see myself as a body but no arms or legs. That's what destroying my balance cells did to me. I just have to wait for impact and suffer the consequences.
>
> 'I don't care about your phone. Are you okay?' he said.
>
> 'Yes,' I said. It was a lie. I was hurt. But I wanted to get up to save face. There were many people on the walking track.
>
> I HATE YOU MENIERE'S!
>
> My husband pulled me up off the ground. My daughter picked up my phone. She was too quiet. How many times

had she witnessed Ménière's bring me to my knees with vertigo, deafness, depression? And now falling.

I blew out a long breath between my lips. Then set a rock in my sights to sit on for a moment to assess my injuries, then walked there, my husband holding onto my arm to support me. I wanted to yell at him, "LET GO OF ME. I'M NOT AN INVALID!" But I didn't. He was trying to help.

I sat on the rock, looked over the lake and focussed on where I hurt – my wrist, my arm, my ankle and my back. Hold yourself together, I thought, people fall all the time. Put on your "I'm okay mask".

'Are you alright, Ma?' my daughter asked.

Hold yourself together. The emotion of "I want to fall to pieces" rolled through me. Hold it together. Breathe.

'It could be worse,' I said, 'I could have broken something.' I was hoping that I didn't break anything. My wrist, arm and ankle were throbbing. Not to mention my back spasms. 'Thanks for picking up my phone,' I added.

She nodded, looking at me with concern in her eyes.

'I'm sorry for falling,' I say to her. I don't want her to be embarrassed by me.

I HATE YOU MENIERE'S!

And of course, she is not. She never is. She's always one of the first to help. It is my own self-judgement that betrays me.

I stand. In pain. But I can walk to finish the last hour of the track.

My daughter is in front of me, glancing back at me every once and a while, and my husband is behind me. I'm glad. He can't see me wriggling my fingers to check my wrist, and feeling where my right arm hurts, nor the wince on my face when my ankle hurts more than I want it to, or my back spasms. All I can think of is when my son would roll his ankle at elite triathlon training, and his coach would tell him to walk normally on it. So that is what I do, despite the pain.

Back at the cafeteria …

'I could have died if I fell in a different part of the walk,' I say. It was true. Parts of the track were on a boardwalk above the ground that fell steeply, scattered with rocks and trees below. No rails to stop a tumble.

'I know,' my husband whispered. I watch his watery eyes and see him swallow harder than usual. 'What do you want to drink? Do you want an ice-cream?' He was using the distraction method. He knows me well.

Claire and I find a table away from most of the people. My wrist and arm throb. My back was spasming and my ankle twinging. Swelling was setting in. I ate my ice-cream, flicking tears from my eyes when they dropped. At least I don't have vertigo, *I thought. It was a good day, after all. Any day without vertigo is a good day.* Suck it up, *I tell myself,* it could be worse.

I have fallen two more times since then. 2022, which I then needed knee surgery for in 2023. And later on in 2023. In the middle of nowhere in Western Australia. No mobile phone service. But God is good. My injuries could have been much worse.

Falling reminds me of Proverbs 24:16:

For though a righteous man falls seven times,
he rises again.

Resilience is one of the blessings of God's incredible human design. It's about being able to adapt to life's misfortunes and setbacks. *Blessed in the mess!*

God's people aren't promised freedom from worldly cares, losses, trials, or attacks of the enemy (*John 16:33; 2 Timothy 2:3; 1 Peter 1:6–7; 5:8*). Even so, the Lord watches over His children (*Psalm 23*). He promises to be with us in our trouble, to deliver us, and honour us (*Psalm 91:15*).

It is said the Godly can expect to encounter trouble and hardship in life. People who do not believe in God also encounter trouble and hardship in life. But having a faith in God is what sets us apart. *Our hope. Our knowing* of our eternal salvation. While non-believers are left searching, scrambling, and floundering on shaky ground in times of hardship, believers stand upon the firm foundations of our faith, and our hope in God.

God works all things together for good.

It doesn't mean we aren't affected by the psychological reactions or physical ailments of the reality of our earthly predicament, we're human, but we can look up, and know that God has got it covered.

When you are in the midst of violent, debilitating vertigo, it makes you question everything. Including the layers of you that you present to others. Your identity. Your *true* identity.

Ménière's disease erased my identity. The person who I thought I *was*. Who I was *known* for. My identity I had built my life on.

The darkness of my Ménière's storm took my identity away. But in that darkness was a pinpoint of Light. God's light. And in it resided my true identity. One that honoured God.

I'm so thankful for everything He has done and will continue to do.

What is *your* identity?

identity
noun

1. the fact of being who or what a person or thing is.
Who or what a person is…

Who are you? Your family? Your lineage?
What do you do for your job?
Your down time? Your alone time?
Does your who are you change, depending on where you are?
Does your what you do change, depending on where you are?
Do you garner your self-confidence on what you do with your life?
Do you consider yourself more or less important because of *what* you do?

Layers …

Each of us wears outer layers to present to others as our identity in society, whether we are aware of it or not. We weren't born with these psychological layers, we cloth ourselves in the layers of identity as we journey through negative and positive experiences in life. Sometimes with pride, sometimes with shame, sometimes to hide our true-selves as a layer of protection.

The culture of our earthly life places emphasis on our identity in *what we do*. In the eyes of others, it will set your position, importance, and worth of you, as a person.

I praise God that He does not see us like that.

When you shed your outer layers—your profession/job, your social class, whether you are a mother/father, a sister/brother, a cousin, an aunty/uncle, your social circles, a neighbour, a disability (if you have one)—who are you now?

Imagine it is just you.

Alone.

Sitting in the middle of a dark, foggy forest.

You are the only one left.

You have no identifying career.

No identifying monetary status.

No identifying social set.

No identifying family.

It's just you, stripped bare from your achievements, everything you have worked hard for, everything you know.

It's just you and your beating heart, and your alert, alarmed mind.

Your true-identity hidden in the darkness, and you know the Light is coming to reveal the true you. It cannot be hidden.

Do you feel at peace, or are you scared?
Do you even like you?
Do you still matter?

At the age of twenty-nine (1995) my symptoms of violent vertigo, tinnitus, fullness of the inner ear, and hearing loss started. Ménière's disease. 0.02% of people around the world have it. No cause. No cure. It's the most liveable disease with the highest suicide rate.

I divide my life into *before* Ménière's disease, and *after*.

Before Ménière's, sport was my passion, and music and art. I was a high achiever in everything I did. Teaching was the career I chose and loved with all my heart. I was that teacher who did the '40-Hour Famine' with students each year and won an award for it. I did 'Jump Rope for Heart' every year with the students, raising money for The Heart Foundation. I ran Scripture Union at lunchtimes, and Skipping Club before school. I was that teacher who always had the other teachers' children in my classes, by request.

I was a "what". I was known by my "what". Over my teaching career I received two nominations for the National Excellence in Teaching Awards for my "what".

But then the unpredictable violent, debilitating vertigo of Ménière's hit. At least 40 times a year. I was incapacitated for three or four hours each time, spinning at an impossible speed, staring at the wall for the entire time trying to cope with what my body was going through, vomiting until the only thing that came up was froth. I was a frequent-flyer at emergency at the hospital for hydration, where I had to educate the doctors and nurses on my incurable disease they had no knowledge of.

I pray that you never experience vertigo like I had.

Eventually, Ménière's took away what I loved to do.

I could no longer participate in sport.
Music was too loud, even though I was going deaf.
Art went by the wayside.
I couldn't teach.
My confidence was stolen.
I was no longer independent.
I couldn't socialise anymore because of my hearing loss and the unpredictability of a vertigo attack.

My food choices were severely limited. Ice was on the menu on some days.

I was underweight.

I lived every conscious moment in fear of an incapacitating vertigo attack. I would even wake in the middle of the night spinning for hours on end.

I became a prisoner in my own home, my own body. Every day was like a battlefield, and the world became very dark.

What was the point of living a life like this?

Each time that I lay staring at the wall, spinning, wherever I was, even the floor in the toilet for four hours because I couldn't be moved during the vertigo, I had no more "what".

It was just me. With nothing. Like a brain with awareness and a decommissioned body experiencing the internal lie that I was spinning, and yet in reality, my physical body wasn't. I was capable of absolutely nothing. I felt like a nothing.

I was a nothing.

I could move my arms and legs, but I couldn't move my head. If I did, it was catastrophic. The spinning was impossibly more terrifying. So, I did the only thing I could—I stared at one spot on a wall for three to four hours, wherever I was, spinning, exhausted from the spinning, the nausea, the vomiting. The only thing left I had was my mind. Me and my mind. Alone. Experiencing a philosophical, theological, existential crisis way before it became a thing.

As I rode the out-of-control spinning merry-go-round, I would imagine myself in heaven, bowing down before God, singing songs of praise with the angels, freed from Ménière's disease with perfect hearing again. It was the only thing that kept me going and Jeremiah 29:11:

> *"For I know the plans I have for you," declares the LORD,*
> *"plans to prosper you and not to harm you, plans to give*
> *you hope and a future."*

As I lay there, rendered defenseless, my life was stripped bare. I was left with my true identity. *I am a child of God.*

As brutal as having Ménière's disease is, I am blessed. It is my constant reminder of God's love for me. It made me realise that small things are big things. It made me search for my blessings and to count them, even in the midst of the darkness when I was on my hands and knees trying to find the missing pieces of my life that had been lost. Without God shining a pinpoint of Light in my internal darkness, I wouldn't be here.

There's a lot more to my journey, but the beautiful thing is, God answered my prayers, in *His way*, and in *His timing*, and He threw in unexpected blessings as well. My story shines with the love and care and mercy of God.

God answers prayers in a way that will blow your mind. He is beyond extravagant!

When we accept our identity as a child of God, it puts a weapon in our hands. *Prayer.*

Who are we? What is our identity?

We are a son or daughter of the Most High. A chosen people. Wonderfully and fearfully made.

According to Ephesians 1, we have been blessed with every spiritual blessing; *we have been chosen, adopted, redeemed, forgiven, grace-lavished and unconditionally loved and accepted. We are pure, blameless and forgiven.* We have received the hope of spending eternity with God. When we are in Christ, these aspects of our identity can never be altered by what we do.

Blessed. Lavished. Forgiven.

I love those words. Verbs. Our identity is in a God of action, of redeeming grace, a loving God who gave his only Son for us.

1 John 3:1:

> *See how much our Father loves us. For he calls us his children, and that is what we are.*

When I was eight-years-old and heard the voice of God for the first time, I was playing in the kitchen beside my brother, taking turns with some tie on roller skates my uncle had given us. My brother kept taking longer turns and I was becoming impatient. I wanted it to be my turn. When I finally got the roller skates off him and revelled in skating on the lino floor of the kitchen, my brother started complaining and said it was his turn.

'Share with your brother, Julie.' The gentle voice didn't command me. It didn't feel or sound scary. It was said in a kind tone like I still had a choice whether to give the roller skates to my brother, *if* I wanted to.

I looked around. My brother and I were the only ones in the kitchen. Dad and Uncle Doug were outside on the verandah.

I needed to know who had spoken to me. So I waked out to

my dad and Uncle Doug, who were leaning over the railing and chatting.

I butted into their conversation. 'Did you say something to me?' I asked.

Dad and Uncle Doug both stopped their conversation and looked at me, like they didn't even know that I was there with them. The both shook their heads and said no.

I returned to the kitchen and replayed what I had heard. 'Share with your brother, Julie.' A voice unlike my dad's voice, or Uncle Doug's. A gentle, guiding voice. Not demanding. I knew then I had heard God's voice. I still had a choice to share with my brother or not.

I chose to listen to God. So I sat next to my brother, took off the roller skates and gave them to my brother, my chest warming because I had followed the voice of God.

God knows what your future is. He knows if you need a nudge, or a voice, to remind you that you are not alone. You just have to listen. He may speak to you personally, or through another person's story. Scripture. A dream. A revelation that opens your eyes to see His immeasurable love, and that you are not alone.

And Jesus... indescribable!

I have overcome the worst symptoms of Ménière's. The vertigo. But I still have hearing loss and tinnitus and my imbalance to remind me of my journey with God and Jesus by my side. I have a cochlear implant now to hear again. Another answered prayer. *God is good.*

> *Psalm 107:1 Give thanks to the LORD, for he is good; his love endures forever.*

I see Ménière's as a blessing. A reminder of God's love. My life is all the more richer for my journey of trusting in our Heavenly Father and praying to him in the name of Jesus.

He sees our tears and bottles them. Psalm 56:8

And this. "My grace is sufficient for you, for my power is made perfect in weakness."

Answered prayers.
One ten years later.
The other 20 years later.
Don't give up praying.

Soli Deo Gloria – All Glory to God Alone

Our now, our present circumstances isn't our forever. There is so much more waiting for us, beyond what we can ever imagine.

Be joyful in hope,
PATIENT IN AFFLICTION,
faithful in prayer

Romans 12:12

His Hands

Heather Davies

As I lie here, wishing I could close my eyes and fall into a deep sleep, I'm held prisoner by an intense spinning sensation. I snuggle under my weighted blanket, it's embrace a welcoming hug. I say a prayer beneath my breath, "Hey Lord, it's me again, it's been a while since my last episode, and I thank you for that. The dizzy-days remind me of my many blessings. Please allow this to pass quickly and help me ride this out gracefully." As I search for a place to set my gaze, I am reminded that His hands are in everything.

My eyes settle in on a great oak just outside my window. Its branches stretching in every direction, a living canopy that shields the brightness of the sun, allowing only gentle bursts of sunlight to peek through. Each branch curves in its imperfectly perfect way, sculpted by storms she survived. Her curves tell a story. Not of weakness, but of endurance, of how strength is often shaped by struggle. Here she stands, stronger and more resilient, *because* the winds and rain pushed against her.

I, too, like the great oak have made it to the other side of every storm. Stronger and more resilient. When my personal storms passed, I often realized a new strength waiting within me. A quiet, steady strength I never realized I had.

Now, as I write, peace washes over me like a gentle wave rolling onto shore. This calmness takes over and reminds me I'm not alone. I never am. He is always with me, wrapping his arms around me, around us just like this gorgeous oak.

The winds will shake each of us but in the stillness that follows, I'm reminded that, His unseen grace always carries us.

My own storms come to mind. I never thought I'd make it through. The many times I felt my faith abandon me, I felt small, insignificant. How many nights had I whispered a quiet prayer, wondering if my faith was enough, even in my weakest moments. I leaned, nauseated and uncertain.

Then a quote from the past, *"faith the size of a mustard seed"*, that's all I needed.

His Grace is enough

In His Hands
Bleu and Nancy Wallace
Parents to *Heather Davies*, The Ménière's Muse

When our daughter, Heather, started to have odd migraine related symptoms and vertigo, the local hospital did a CT and it showed a small tumor in her head. She was referred to *Mayo Clinic* in Jacksonville, Florida. I drove her there several times, the four hour, one-way drive. We were so worried about her and her health, having a small child, Lyla and teenage son, Devon.

The hospital was excellent and it seemed to take a group of physicians from several specialties to diagnose of vestibular migraine and Ménière's disease. These terrible diseases include nausea, dizziness, hearing issues, tinnitus and awful migraines.

We did a lot of praying to our Lord to release her from this problem, or at the very least give her the strength to survive it. She has not only survived, she has started back to work again.

Her father and I have come to believe she has turned to Jesus more in her life than we could have hoped, due to her illness.

I know, and can tell as her faith grew, she has too. We are very proud of our lovely, loving daughter, and *thank Him* for giving her to us.

Fear Not, For I Am With You

Jenny Chaves

In December 2020, my life changed overnight, unfortunately for the worse! I suddenly lost hearing in my right ear, followed that night by a violent episode of rotational vertigo. I woke up spinning, vomiting, and completely terrified! I had no idea what was happening to me.

At first, I thought it was really bad food poisoning or a terrible ear infection. But all my symptoms had gone away by the next day, so I wasn't too worried about what had happened to me. However, this intense experience was always in the back of my mind because I knew whatever it was it was something scary and serious.

After telling a good friend of mine what had happened to me, she encouraged me to make an appointment with an ENT. By then (months later) my hearing had temporarily returned, so I was shocked when the doctor told me I had mild hearing loss! Especially because I always had perfect hearing ability and I was only forty-three years old.

Then after I described my crazy vertigo episode to the doctor he immediately ordered a brain MRI and several blood tests because he said what was happening to me was highly unusual. I was scared, but grateful when the results showed no tumors on my brain MRI.

Still, the doctor suspected possible Ménière's disease (MD) and/or Lyme disease as my diagnosis. I already knew what Lyme disease was, however, I did not know anything about MD, so I looked it up online on Dr. Google. Big mistake!

All the descriptions overwhelmed me—people call it "the worst disease you can have without being terminally ill".

I cried every day for months considering I might have Ménière's. Until this point, I had never truly known depression. But losing my hearing, experiencing multiple vertigo attacks, and feeling my body spiraling out of control left me incredibly anxious and afraid.

Each day I would drive to my favorite spot by the river and weep, asking God, "Why me?"

I had been a believer in Christ since childhood, thanks to my parents and the youth group I grew up in. But over the years, my faith had unfortunately slipped quietly to the background.

When our daughter was born in 2019, life became so much more purposeful and wonderful, but also even busier. Now, while battling Ménière's disease, I was also caring for a newborn who we had recently adopted. It was the most beautiful and most stressful period of my entire life, and I didn't know where to turn.

A sweet friend invited me to her church, and that invitation became a turning point. The beautiful worship music touched my heart, reignited my faith, and brought me to tears.

At home, I began listening to Christian music again - especially songs like "Hills and Valleys" by *Tauren Wells*. The lyrics spoke to my pain:

"When I'm walking through the valley, I know I am not alone.
You're God of the hills and valleys—and I am not alone."

In the years after my diagnosis, I also endured other health issues from failed back surgery and a sudden massive stroke after I received the COVID vaccine in 2021. It felt like I had hit rock bottom with all my medical problems and unfortunately, this is when my Ménière's started ramping up. And to make things worse, after yet another hearing test, my ENT told me that I had quickly progressed to being profoundly deaf in my right ear!

I was on disability, not working, and seeing multiple doctors, including an ENT, a neurotologist, a neurologist, a pain management physician, and a psychiatrist - all of which prescribed a long list of medications. At one point I was on twelve different medications!!! The medications treated my symptoms, but not the root cause of my disease.

With God's grace, in 2025, I eventually tapered off nearly all of the medications, including all psychiatric medications (except two - a diuretic & vestibular suppressant), and began to feel *much* better, and so much more like myself again.

One of the hardest lessons I've learned is, that I'm not in control of my body. Ménière's disease often feels like a reckless driver taking over the wheel and flipping my life upside down at any given moment.

Yet through prayer, music, supportive friends, time in nature, and activities that lift my spirit, I have thankfully found ways to cope.

Living with a chronic invisible illness is very traumatic. I was recently told by a neuropsychologist that I actually have PTSD from Ménière's disease. To say the least, hearing loss, tinnitus, vertigo, and dizziness are exhausting - especially when you must lean on your spouse to care for both your child and yourself.

It's a tough road, but I'm living proof that you can survive. *God is always there*, walking beside you, even when you can't see Him.

One of my favorite poems is *"Footprints in the Sand."* It tells of a person walking along the beach with the Lord. In the hardest moments of life, there's only one set of footprints—not because God left, but because He was carrying them.

Looking back now, I see that God has been carrying me, too.

After one failed adoption, God blessed us with our miracle daughter who we were lucky enough to adopt as an infant in October, 2019. God knew that after the trials I would face ahead with my health issues and miscarriages that I would need my daughter just as much as she needed me! She is the light of my life and the reason I wake up every day. She brings so much happiness and joy into my life. I honestly don't know what I do without her and my husband.

So another message I have is… "Don't ever give up on your dreams no matter how hard the road gets!"

Thankfully, my husband accepts me with my medical issues, which I know is hard for him, but very amazing of him! I am forever grateful to him for sticking by my side through thick and thin. So also, *please don't give up on your dream of having a relationship or getting married*, because there are people out there who are willing to be with you despite your illness! God gave me a loving husband, family, and wonderful friends, who are incredibly supportive - so I feel blessed in many ways.

To anyone fighting Ménière's disease, or any chronic battle: things can get better. *Don't give up. Give your struggles to God* - He will never fail you. Even if you don't see it at first, He's always there, loving you and working for your good.

This illness has taught me to appreciate the smallest blessings I'm gifted by God everyday… like waking up without nausea or vertigo, being able to drive, being able to walk, being able to do the dishes and clean the house, and being able to take care of my daughter. There are so many things people take for granted everyday, which I have a much greater appreciation for now! Because, when I'm at my sickest, I can't do even the most basic things, which can be very disheartening.

I've also learned how to adapt by using my hearing aids. My sweet father bought me new technology called XRAI (AI live transcription glasses). These super cool eyeglasses display the words people are saying in real-time directly in front of them on the lenses of your glasses, so you can read what they are saying!

I mean, how cool is that!

In the future, I may need to get a cochlear implant, but I'm holding off for as long as possible, as long as the hearing in my better left ear doesn't get any worse. These are some of the technologies that help me to stay connected and communicate better, but my true strength comes from inside… *my faith.*

God is my greatest advocate, but I've also learned the importance of advocating for myself and finding the *best* doctors who will battle this monster of a disease with you.

DON'T EVER give up!!!

Fight for your health, and your life, and don't lose hope, you are not alone. Every moment you are alive is worth living! Just keep searching for the sunlight through the trees.

Closing Message

Despite my physical traumas and losses, my faith has grown deeper and stronger. My story isn't about what I've endured—it's about how Jesus Christ has carried me through it all and blessed me with so many wonderful, unexpected miracles in my life. And he can do the same for you. Like my favorite song says, *"No matter where you are—on the mountain or in the valley—you are not alone!"*

My Four Favorite Bible Verses that Give Hope and Strength

Isaiah 41:10

Fear not, for I am with you; be not dismayed, for I am your God; I will strengthen you, I will help you, I will uphold you with my righteous right hand.

Joshua 1:9 is a Bible verse that encourages strength and courage, stating:

Have I not commanded you? Be strong and courageous. Do not be afraid; do not be discouraged, for the LORD your God will be with you wherever you go.

It's a promise of God's presence to provide strength and support to those who follow His commands, particularly in the face of challenges.

Philippians 4:6–7

Do not be anxious about anything, but in every situation, by prayer and petition, with thanksgiving, present your requests to God. And the peace of God, which transcends all understanding, will guard your hearts and your minds in Christ Jesus.

Isaiah 35:5

The ears of the deaf shall be unstopped.

Context and Meaning

A Prophecy of Restoration:

Isaiah 35 is a vision of a flourishing desert landscape, which symbolizes the spiritual renewal brought about by the coming of the Messiah and the establishment of God's reign.

Healing of Disabilities:

The verse highlights the supernatural healing of physical ailments, stating that blindness and deafness will be overcome. This foreshadows the future reign of Jesus Christ, who performed such miracles.

Fulfilling a Promise:

This prophecy is seen as a foretelling of the miraculous events that occurred when Jesus was on Earth, such as when he "opened" the ears and tongue of a deaf man.

Symbolic Significance:

While the verse refers to physical healing, it also carries a deeper spiritual meaning, representing how the spiritual blindness and deafness of humanity to God's truths would be removed.

God's Love for Us is Amazing!

David Giugno

Christmas Eve, 2014.

The day when my life changed forever.

It was a normal day just like any other day. I went to work in the morning. At 4am, I went to sing in the church choir and was planning on going back at 7pm to sing again. I went home to grab something to eat before going back to church because we had some family over. They bought Chinese food which I ate, and all of a sudden, the life I had changed in a minute.

It changed forever.

I had my first vertigo attack.

The room was spinning.

I couldn't stand.

I thought I was dying.

I didn't know what was going on with me.

The next day I woke up and I felt like crap but the vertigo was gone. But then I kept having more attacks, and went to the doctor. It took three years before I was diagnosed with Ménière's disease.

It changed my life forever.

I couldn't work anymore. I am totally deaf in my left ear and partially deaf on my right. It's been a struggle but in a lot of ways, it's been a blessing, and I say this because there's things I've learned, and things I've learned about myself.

I learned that I was stronger than I've ever been in my life. *Mentally*. Not physically. And I'm a much better person that I had ever been in those first fifty-four years of being on this earth before my first vertigo attack. A much better husband, father... *everything*, you name it.

I've learned to embrace my disability, not say, "God why me?" But it's still a challenge. Ménière's disease is a challenge.

Every day is a challenge.

Every day that I wake up that's a good day, is a blessing.

What changed? I decided to be better. I also decided to help other people with Ménière's disease.

I'm in a lot of Ménière's disease support groups on Facebook, and founded *Ménière's and Vertigo with Christian Borders* and *Ménière's and Vertigo Without Borders.*

I often see that people think that God is punishing them by giving them an incurable ear disease. "What kind of a God does this?"

2018 saw me thinking the same thing. And I've been a Catholic my whole life! I've always gone to church. But it would ebb and flow.

In 2018, I really hit rock bottom. It was the year I had to stop working. Retiring at age fifty-one. I mean, that is kind of unheard of, and I know there are people younger than me that have retired due to their own circumstances. But with this, I really starting thinking to myself, *God doesn't like me. God's punishing me. Why is He doing this?* And I really took a turn down.

After a long road, I decided to have some therapy and take some medication just to keep me afloat. For a couple of years, I was still going to church, but when I went, it was like I was there physically,

but spiritually, mentally, I was somewhere else. I really was.
Then COVID came.

COVID hit and everything shut down. The priest in my parish at that time, *Father Fran O'Brien*, called me up and he said, "Hey Dave, I know you're the church photographer, do you think you could do video?"

And I said, "Yeah, sure I can do that!" But I had no clue. I didn't know what I was doing. I grabbed the camera that I had and made the first video. And after a while, after a couple of months, it was around when Easter was starting, the Holy season, Holy Week, the time when we were doing the Holy Thursday services and I remember, it just clicked in my head, the moment after the last supper when Jesus went to Gethsemane to pray and he said,

"My Father, if it is possible, may this cup

be taken from me. Yet not as I will, but as you will."

That really registered with me, and that was when everything started clicking again, and it's like, okay, Jesus accepted what God had in front of Him, that whole thing you know, the trial - six hours of torment and pain and suffering and died and rose three days later. But he accepted it. He didn't think God didn't love him. He accepted it because he knew that's what God wanted.

So that's when things started clicking with me and I'm like, *wait a minute, this is what Gina has been telling me and it's taking me two years to understand what she was saying and it took this one thing, that on line in the Bible, in the gospel!*

And that's when my *YouTube* channel started, because now, it's like, I know what I have to do. I have to try to help other people more than just in this small community of support groups that I founded, but worldwide, and that's when things took off.

Jesus did what God wanted. He didn't do what He wanted.

So this is what God wants me to do. And I'm not going to say it's been easy because it's not. It's never easy.

This year alone (2025), I've had two ear surgeries. I had sac decompression to relieve the vertigo. *Thank you, Lord.* And now, the cochlear implant, and my overall hearing now is so much better than it's been in over ten years. So things have improved.

But there has still been downs, like when my daughter-in-law passed away from COVID, leaving my son with two little kids. They moved in with us and we take care of them, and that can be very frustrating at times because let's face, it I'm fifty-nine. My wife is sixty-three, and we're raising kids again.

My faith is never gone. I pray every day and now, when I go to church, I'm there physically and mentally. I'm in the church, or if I watch it on TV, which I do everyday, I'm there. I'm focused.

But there is still an ebb and flow.

Earlier this year I went to confession, but it was just a habit as I had to pick up the mics I left behind. I left them there but I knew I could get into the church on a Wednesday night even though I don't have a key to the church.

This particular time I just happened to walk in on a Penance service. And I sat down. Normally I don't go to confession, and then I thought, *well, God's talking to me again,* and I went to confession and my faith really, really jumped up.

After that I've been so much better since.

So remember something. God didn't give your condition to you. God wants to know what you're going to do with it.

Are you going to help people?

Are you going to become a VeDa Ambassador?

Are you going to start a blog?

Are you going to participate in support groups?

Are you going to give more than you take?

How are you going to give?

Are you going to pray for people?

That's the way it's always been with Christians. It's not how much you can get. It's *how much you can give.*

And that's what I do.

Back in 2014, Christmas Eve, I could have said *bah humbug, this day changed my life, and I hate it.* But I don't. I take it as - *this day changed my life.* Yes, I have challenges, but my life is a lot better than what it used to be, and I am very happy about that.

John 6:38 – 40

Not My will, but the will of the One who sent Me.

Ménière's and Faith

Julieann Wallace

Faith
complete trust or confidence in someone

I love this quote:
"What gives me the most hope every day is God's grace; knowing that His grace is going to give me the strength for whatever I face, knowing that nothing is a surprise to God." - Rick Warren

My family never went to church. My family never discussed God, or Jesus, or prayed. But here I was, the introverted girl with the quiet God and Jesus belief, who grew into the introverted teenager with the quiet God and Jesus belief, who grew into the woman with the quiet God and Jesus belief, and a strong faith.

Never in my life would I have predicted that I needed that belief in God and Jesus to carry me through the storm of Ménière's disease, and my life, in general.

God whispers. Listen for Him.

One Monday while on holidays in the north of Australia, Cairns, I watched some fearless people build their hang gliders at the top of a cliff for hours before finally taking flight. Amongst them was a woman in her 40s, moving around full of confidence, building her hang glider to prepare to jump off the cliff to catch the uplift of the wind and fly in freedom. She looked like she had jumped off the cliff with her hang glider wings a hundred times.

She re-checked the integrity of her hang glider, lined it up near the edge of the cliff, and spotted her direction of takeoff.

I thought, *how brave! How inspiring!* I couldn't wait to watch her soar into the sky.

It reminded me of having faith in God, and taking a leap of faith, trusting God that the outcome would be good.

Then I watched her falter more times than I could count, each time right before take-off. Fighting the fear. Trying to step out of her comfort zone, but being unable to.

I curiously watched as other hang gliders gathered around her and talked her through take off.

Words of encouragement.

Support.

It reminded me of when people are struggling in life, and with life, and how God sends the helpers. Remember that person who helped you once, or twice, or more?

I like to call them God's rescue packages, and God glitters. They come in the form of people, but also as animals, nature, words from the Bible.

I've also discovered that God may bless you with talents you had no idea you possessed, to open and use at the appointed time.

God is so gracious. With a love that is incomprehensible to us.

As I watched the woman struggling to take flight, it got me thinking, can you have trust without faith?

Are they independent of each other?

Or do they work together?

Or does one build the other?

And then it reminded me of my life. A–B. *Easy* right. I have a plan. I am at A, and I know how to get to B.

Simple.

Done.

When I was little, I wanted to be Batman.

This was not God's plan!

By the time I was nine, I wanted to be a nun because I loved God so much.

This was also not God's plan!

When I attended primary and high school, my favourite parts of the day were morning tea, lunch time, going home and school holidays. Teaching could never have been in God's plan…

But guess what. I became a teacher, even though I was that student in high school who was way too introverted to answer questions in class, and told my friend sitting next to me the answers, who then gave the answer to the class, and the teacher thought *she* was really smart. I would just look down and smile meekly.

Outside of school, sport, music and art were my passions. Every afternoon. Every weekend.

After I accepted the mission of teaching, the plan was to be married, have children (before I lost all my patience on kids at school) and teach until retirement.

Simple.

Clear cut.

No bumps.

No obstacles.

Life's a breeze.

A straight line from A to B!

People who knew me and the life I presented to them said how perfect my life was. How everything just seemed to fall into place.

In reality, what they didn't see, what was hidden from them, is like a messy scribble on paper and in my mind—teaching, and throw in facial paralysis at twenty-seven years of age (Bell's Palsy), Ménière's disease from twenty-nine (violent vertigo, tinnitus, deafness, ear fullness), three children (*a blessing*), deep dark depression due to Ménière's disease, in a very bad place trying to find the missing pieces of me, thinking of ending my life, balance cells destroyed to stop the vertigo (*answered prayer*), relearning to walk using my sight for balance, becoming an author (never expected that in a million years!), having a cochlear implant and relearning to hear again (*answered prayer*), being a research subject at the *University of Queensland's* Mind and Brain Centre to help people with Ménière's disease, three times.

You know the seasons of life, Biblically? The tumultuous storm with my Ménière's disease is definitely my very long winter season. I like to call it the *Woe of Winter*, as opposed to the *Echo of Autumn*, the *Bloom of Spring*, and the *Melody of Summer*.

But through my woe of winter, when I look back, God was there. Watching over me. Even though it didn't feel like it at the time.

"Often times God demonstrates His faithfulness in adversity by providing for us what we need to survive. He does not change our painful circumstances. He sustains us through them." (Charles Stanley)

You know what really gets me about that quote? It's talking about God's faithfulness to us, not the other way around. It just makes me go, 'WOW!'

In *my* life journey, I've learned this from God's plan:
- *Don't judge others.* You don't know what they have been

through, or are going through. *Be kind!*
- *God is always there, even when you think he is not.* Do NOT start to believe the lies that you are unworthy, or you must be so bad that you deserve all of this.
- *Trust* in his plan. His plan is *far more exciting,* offering you opportunities beyond your imagination.
- *He sends gifts to open when you least expect it*, physical and spiritual - when you are in a low place you think you can't get out of – He sends bible verses, people, the beauty of nature, and for me, writing to escape from my reality of no balance, extremely loud tinnitus, deafness. I penned *The Colour Of Broken,* under a pen name, Amelia Grace (Grace being God's grace) with a main character Ménière's disease, who also has a strong, never-ending faith in God, written to bring awareness to Ménière's disease, so I could be a voice for those to finally be heard and understood. The novel was long-listed twice to be made into a movie, and hit #1 on Amazon numerous time. *Praise to God.*
- He speaks to you. *God whispers.* Sometimes He sends dreams, like in 2000, when I was in a very dark place with Ménière's ... *in the dream*, I was sitting in Darlene Zschech's church (which she didn't have at the time. Darlene's and Mark's church, *HopeUC*, opened in January 2011). Darlene was preaching and called me up to speak on stage, which I had no idea was going to happen—instant speaking-in-public-fear filled me—all I remember thinking was that God would give me the right words to speak - *Luke 12:12 - The Holy Spirit will give you the words to say at the moment when you need them.* I walked to the stage to speak to a couple of hundred people and said, *'We live in the moment, and can't see beyond our struggles. God sees you and what you*

are going through. He sees your whole life, from beginning to end. This is where you are right now,' I said, spreading my hands apart to show about 20 centimetres (7 inches) in length, *'in this moment in time, compared to this.'* I spread my hands as far apart as I could. *'It will get better.'*

I shared my dream with a friend who was going through a difficult time with chronic fatigue, even though it was a message for me and my suffering. My friend wrote me a letter a year later, saying what I shared with her changed her path and her chronic fatigue was gone. Twenty years after that dream, 2020, Darlene asked to interview me about my Ménière's journey and faith on *Instagram live*. Again, I thought, *God will give me the words*. I did prepare beforehand as Darlene had sent me the questions she might ask, which took some pressure off. But this time, it wasn't around 200 people I would be speaking to like in her church, she had 440, 000 followers at the time.

God speaks in the silence of the heart - Mother Teresa

In 2022, four weeks before my father died, I had a dream that someone was visiting the family. I was outside on a road. The day was lovely. I put my arm around that person and said, 'I'm glad you're here, he doesn't have much earth time left.'

On the 22nd June, 2022, Dad was admitted to hospital. The doctors where going to adjust his medications to take the load off his heart so he would feel better. In the afternoon, Mum and I left the hospital to go home to get some clothes for him. As I was walking out of the hospital rooms, I heard in my mind, *go back and talk to your father*. Three times. But I ignored it. I knew exactly why I had to go back and talk to my dad. It was to have a conversation with him about God and Jesus, before it was too late. And I ignored it.

I wrestled with my lack of courage to go back and speak with my dad all afternoon and into the night. Overwhelmed with worry that I was going to be too late to see him the next day and had lost the opportunity that, I called my eldest son and asked him to call Grampy and talk to him and pray with him. Declan said the phone call kept cutting out and he didn't get to pray with him.

I was devastated.

As I lay in bed that night, I made the decision to go to see Dad at the hospital first thing in the morning, regardless of the visiting times. It felt like a race against time. Dad's earth time.

As I was driving to the hospital, I asked God to put the right words in my mouth to talk to Dad about Him and his Son, and rehearsed in the car how to talk to Dad about God and Jesus, and whether he believed in them, and to talk to him about heaven. In the car my conversation with Dad was so smooth and wonderful.

It wasn't the first time that I had talked to my Dad about what he believed, because I thought that his time was near for quite a few years. The last time I talked about God to my dad, my kids were there. Me, Dad and my three kids. I asked Dad whether he believed in God. He shook his head and said, 'I don't know what I believe.'

My eldest son handed him his favourite leather bound Bible and said, 'Grampy, start reading from Mark.' But he never did.

And that was it.

When I arrived at Dad's hospital bed, he was sitting up with all the beeps and alarms you hear in the emergency department. He was smiling at me.

On my way, walking to his bed I was stressing about how to bring up the conversation I needed to have.

'You're here early,' he said.

'Mum told me your phone wasn't working.'

'Sometimes it does but other times it doesn't. Declan called me this morning and he was saying something but I couldn't hear him.' I thought, *that was him trying to pray for you.*

Dad didn't hear it. But I was here now. This was my calling to do for Dad. And my honour.

'Let me look at your phone,' I said.

Dad handed me his phone. I sat down and started to look at it, but I was bursting with "I need to talk with you words".

And out it tumbled. 'Dad. I'm going to heaven and I want to see you there when I get there. I need to know if you believe in God?' These words fell out of my mouth like they had been in a tumble dryer. So much for the smooth delivery I had practised in the car.

He nodded his head. 'Yes,' he said.

'And Jesus? Do you believe in Jesus?'

Dad nodded his head. 'Yes. I always have. But nothing is going to happen to me,' he said.

In my mind I heard, *yes it is*.

'And,' I said, 'you know when you pass away, you are not alone. The angels are there waiting for you.'

Dad nodded. And I knew I had said enough.

That afternoon, while Dad was waiting for a transfer to another hospital to potentially get a heart pacemaker, Dad lifted his left hand to his head and said, 'I've got a pain in my head.' And then his eyes rolled back and the alarms went off.

There was a rush of frantic activity around Dad while the nurses worked on him, and Mum and I were quickly ushered out of the room. Despite all their efforts, Dad's last chapter on earth had ended.

Mum and I were brought back into his room. I went on one side of Dad, and Mum the other, and I prayed for Dad. And I prayed for my mum and for God's grace and love and comfort for her to carry her through the exceptionally difficult days ahead.

And then came the shock. The numbness. The sobbing. Me witnessing my beautiful mum screaming out at my dad to speak to her. My Mum trying to climb onto his bed and pleading for him to take her with him...

But I knew. God's timing is always right.

Trust God.

John 3:36 Whoever believes in the Son has eternal life.

When I was in the midst of my violent, frequent vertigo attacks in my thirties, I struggled with "why me?". My wings felt like they had been clipped and I was grounded, and I was not allowed to reach my potential or dreams.

Each time that I lay staring at the wall, spinning, wherever I was, even on the floor in the toilet for four hours because I couldn't be moved during the vertigo, I felt like I had no more 'what'. What was my life supposed to be? What was my career or job supposed to be? I couldn't work. What was my purpose?

It was just me. With nothing. Like a brain with awareness and a decommissioned body experiencing the internal lie that I was spinning, and yet in reality, my physical body wasn't. I was capable of absolutely nothing. I felt like a nothing. I was a nothing.

I could move my arms and legs, but I couldn't move my head. If I did, it was catastrophic. The spinning was impossibly more terrifying. So, I did the only thing I could—I stared at one spot on a wall for three to four hours, wherever I was, spinning, exhausted from the spinning, the nausea, the vomiting. The only thing left

I had was my mind. Me and my mind. Alone. Experiencing a philosophical existential crisis, way before it became a thing.

As I rode the out of control spinning merry-go-round, I would imagine myself in heaven, bowing down before God, singing songs of praise with the angels, freed from Ménière's disease with perfect hearing again. That kept me going, and Jeremiah 29:11:

> *"For I know the plans I have for you," declares the Lord,*
> *"plans to prosper you and not to harm you,*
> *plans to give you hope and a future."*

The only thing I had left as my life was stripped bare, was my true-identity. I am a child of God.

As brutal as having Ménière's disease is, I am blessed. It is my constant reminder of God's love for me. It made me realise that small things are big things. It made me search for my blessings and to count them, even in the midst of the darkness when I was on my hands and knees trying to find the pieces of my life that had been lost. Without God shining a pinpoint of Light in my internal darkness, I wouldn't be here.

There's a lot more to my journey, but the beautiful thing is, God answered my prayers, in *His way*, and in *His timing*, and He threw in unexpected blessings as well.

God answers prayers in a way that will blow your mind. All you need to do is ask. He listens. He is extravagant!

According to Ephesians 1, *we have been blessed with every spiritual blessing; we have been chosen, adopted, redeemed, forgiven, grace-lavished and unconditionally loved and accepted. We are pure, blameless and forgiven. We have received the hope of spending eternity with God. When we are in Christ, these aspects of our identity can never be altered by what we do.*

Blessed.

Lavished.

Forgiven.

I love those words. Verbs. Our identity is in a God of action, of redeeming grace, a loving God who gave his only Son for us.

I am not a "what". I am a "who".

Did I pray for healing in my Ménière's journey?

Absolutely. Sooo many times. *And* heard a "No!"

And so I accepted it. But God didn't answer my prayer according to what I wanted. He had something way better than I could ever have imagined.

I had to learn trust.

Do I look at my Ménière's as a punishment? No. I look at my Ménière's as a reminder of God's love for me. I look at how many times He guided me out of the darkness. How many times Jesus carried me through the impossibly difficult days. How many times He has given me the feeling of peace, when I should have been a ball of messy, ugly stress.

He never leaves us. God's got this.

Trust Him in the storm.

Thank Him and praise Him in all the kinds of unpredictable days - chaotic, messy, beautiful, tough, even those days that seem unbearable. He sends us God whispers and God glitters and unexpected rescue packages. Look back at your journey and you will see them.

That afternoon of watching people take leaps of faith off the cliff with hang gliding, I caught a plane back to Brisbane with my husband. I remember looking down at the earth from way above the clouds, and in a clear patch of sky, my breath caught by how we are invisible from a distance. It's like we don't even exist.

But to God, we are His *everything*.

We matter.
We belong.
We are loved.
He sees us. He hears us.
And He *will* deliver us from our troubles.
And it will be more magnificent than you can ever imagine!
I am a daughter of God. *And that is all that I need.*
His grace is sufficient for me.

James 1:12

Blessed is the one who perseveres under trial because, having stood the test, that person will receive the crown of life that the Lord has promised to those who love him.

Faith
MAKES ALL THINGS POSSIBLE

In Sickness & In Health

Angela Selar

1 Corinthians 13:4-8 (New International Version)

"Love is patient, love is kind. It does not envy, it does not boast, it is not proud. It does not dishonor others, it is not self-seeking, it is not easily angered, it keeps no record of wrongs. Love does not delight in evil but rejoices with the truth. It always protects, always trusts, always hopes, always perseveres. Love never fails".

As a life-long, severe, chronic, multiple diagnosis vestibular issue patient of over five decades at the publishing of this book, I can say I have experience many of life's highs and lows in my share of relationships. I was a wife for decades and now a widow, a parent of two young adults, have life long friends of 40 and 50 years. My children and closest friends have been my rock along with my mother, who also has Meniere's. Rest her soul. I thank them for their patience and understanding.

    I was diagnosed at age thirteen with bilateral Meniere's, Vestibular Migraine, and have had multiple Cholesteatoma removals with rebuilds. Many additional vestibular issues have always loomed. I hear with middle ear implants and have mixed hearing loss with constant tinnitus and severe almost daily vertigo bouts.

Despite all this, I have live a happy, peaceful life, weathering this storm, by focusing on positive purpose, perspective, and living in the present through gratitude. I thank the Dear Lord daily for all the preciousness I have in my life. There is much that is precious to see, even in storms.

Vestibular disorders can be difficult for all relationships. It doesn't matter whether marriage, friendship, siblings, children, parents coworkers acquaintances, neighbors or just the general public. Even a mild vestibular issue can adversely impact, changing the dynamics of the relationship. People are not creatures of change.

A patient who lives with an active severe vestibular disorder like Vestibular Migraine/Ménière's Disease (especially together which is 56% for unilateral and 85% of Ménière's patients) live with the same quality of life rating on basic depression and pain clinical assessments as a person six days from death with cancer or AIDs (Anderson JP, Harris JP. Impact of Ménière's disease on quality of life. https://pmc.ncbi.nlm.nih.gov/articles/PMC4069154/). Vestibular patients don't die. We must live on and try to make a happy and peaceful life. How do we weather this storm? Considering that when females have cancer, the divorce rate is 20.8%, compared to only 2.9% for males, one may ask what impact a severe vestibular disorder can have on my marriage, let alone other relationships (https://pubmed.ncbi.nlm.nih.gov/19645027/).

1 Corinthians 13:4-8 talks about love and what it is. It's a guide of things to remember in weathering life's storms. In marriage, this passage is popular as a reading during the ceremony.

But it's message can be forgotten within the marriage in day-to-day living, especially when your communicating ability becomes taxed due to hearing loss, or a person is not able to do what they have always done around the house daily, or a loss of financial stability, or participation in family and social events, etc., due to the chronic nature of severe vestibular issues. In marriage, it is not just the sick spouse who's life changes! The whole dynamics of both parties life do. This can be especially difficult if a vestibular patient is young and the lifestyle ends up not matching between the spouses. Resentment can run high. Empathy can run short. People who have never experienced vertigo just may not, "Get it." Being able to live day to day with another person peacefully is important.

How do you weather this storm?

#1. Realize that it is not only the unwell spouse who is learning to manoeuvre, cope, and adjust. Both people in the relationship need to understand that a chronic illness affects both of them greatly in everyday living. Simple things like dishes, laundry, attention to kids and dinner can become sources of strife. How do you weather this storm?

> *"Love is patient, love is kind. It does not envy, it does not boast, it is not proud. It does not dishonor others, it is not self-seeking, it is not easily angered, it keeps no record of wrongs. Love does not delight in evil but rejoices with the truth. It always protects, always trusts, always hopes, always perseveres. Love never fails."*

Possible answer: Commitment between the two people to try

their best to follow and live true to *1 Corinthians 13:4-8*. Both people, not just one, have to work to live by this simple guidance that the Bible gives.

Be patient. We as humans do not always understand. *Listen for understanding, not just respond to best communication.* People listen to respond, not listen for understanding and comprehending. Much gets lost when you do not *actively* listen for understanding and comprehension.

Be kind in your words and actions, always, not only to your partner but also *yourself.*

Do not envy for what another can do but especially, do not envy what you used to be able to do before the vestibular issues hit.

Acknowledging, accommodating and learning to live with the life changes of a chronic vestibular issue and it's dynamics in a healthy, targeted way, produces the best results in relationships.

Acknowledge: Both parties in a marriage or relationship experience the *stages of grief* in adjusting to living with a severe vestibular disorder, especially when it hits in the younger years. When people marry, people talk about life plans. They dream or a wonderful life. But a severe vestibular disorder throws a monkey wrench into those life plans. *Long term* is a long time. It's important to understand the stages of grief, because people with chronic illness do go through the stages of grief, and knowing each of these stages can help ease the mental load. *Give yourself and others grace.*

Communication: Many times with a severe chronic vestibular disorder, hearing loss accompanies it. Hearing loss alone, without vertigo, is difficult within relationships! Living with someone who has hearing loss can be difficult if you are not used to it.

> *"Love is patient, love is kind. It does not envy, it does not boast, it is not proud. It does not dishonor others, it is*

not self-seeking, it is not easily angered, it keeps no record of wrongs. Love does not delight in evil but rejoices with the truth. It always protects, always trusts, always hopes, always perseveres. Love never fails."

Accommodations: Grief counseling/marriage counseling/individual mental patient care is important to long term outcomes in chronic severe vestibular disorder patients. We tend to not drive, go places, or like being in crowds of people. Our world shrinks.

In my childhood, I went to a religious primary school. My faith is bound to that experience. In marriage, I took the vow of, "In sickness and in health," deeply to heart, especially because I had a chronic, life-long illness. In doing so, it helped me to weather the storms of life on solid ground. *1 Corinthians 13:4-8* gave me tools to use to educate my spouse in healthy ways in my illnesses. Reading it each morning kept me focused on my marriage, family and God's blessings in our lives. His blessings and lessons have helped me to weather this storm.

On the Other Side

Christine Moyer

As single mom, working full-time, attending graduate school at night, I became a master at carefully balancing an overwhelmed life until I was bedridden from chronic dizziness, physically and emotionally sliding into a dark valley with no end in sight.

For a brief moment, I sat down in the valley. Full of despair, I asked God, "Why me? I can't live like this, Lord, please take me home."

Then God reminded me, "David did not sit in the valley. David did not run through the valley. He walked through it with God's protection and guidance."

Psalm 23:4

> *"Even though I walk through the valley of the shadow of death, I will fear no evil, for you are with me; your rod (protection) and your staff (guidance), they comfort me."*

The valley is not a dead end! The valley, without sun and full of clouds, is a temporary place. The other side may look different. The experience may have changed you forever. But we don't unpack and set up camp in the valley. We walk, one step at a time, with God's protection and guidance until we see the sun on the other side.

Christine Moyer was diagnosed with PPPD in 2022. Christine, known as 'thatdizzzygirl' on social media, started her platform to spread hope and awareness about vestibular disorders. She now serves on the Board of Directors of the Vestibular Disorders Association raising funds for vestibular research, speaking to raise awareness, and advocate for vestibular patients. Christine returned to work full-time as a special education teacher with plans of completing graduate school in 2026 with her daughter by her side.

chosen
BLESSED
♡ *forgiven* ♡
REDEEMED

Art

Exodus 35:31-33

*He has filled him with the Spirit of God,
in wisdom and understanding,
in knowledge and all manner of workmanship,
to design artistic works,
to work in gold and silver and bronze,
in cutting jewels for setting,
in carving wood,
and to work in all manner
of artistic workmanship.*

You
Lisa K. Champion
Ménière's diagnosed in 2007
Photography

When I saw the rays of light coming down upon the sunflower, I thought of how God watches over me from above. When I'm having a bad day with my Ménière's disease, or one of my other illnesses, He wraps His arms around me and comforts me and doesn't leave my side. I'm thankful that when I put the guitar down and picked up this camera and started taking pictures that He opened my eyes. The world is really beautiful and I'm just lucky to be the girl behind the lens to show you how beautiful it can be.

Instagram/photogrl.lisak

Resilience

My name is *Kathleen Ney*. I was diagnosed with Ménière's disease in 1999 and now have bilateral disease with Vestibular Migraine. I have worked as a professional artist for many years. I hope that my images touch people and communicate some of the beauty and wonder of life on earth.

In nature, I experience a divine source energy that can be seen and felt. I draw much inspiration from the large trees of the American Pacific Northwest rain forest, which can be seen as symbols of the link between heaven and earth. There are so many challenges having bilateral MD, as well as the inevitable losses of getting older. So I look to the trees as a conduit of the Creator's energy, put my feet on their roots and ask for strength and stability.

These two *Resilience* paintings were done this year while dealing with the storms of illness. Even when buffeted by the elements, the trees' persistence to deal with whatever comes, gives me hope.

God's Romance
Julieann Wallace
Acrylic paint on canvas
50 x 50cm

God's Romance explores the majestic craftsmanship of a loving King in heaven who wants to share his overflowing love and provision with all of us. Flowers are a symbol of beauty, of appreciation, of love. Flowers tell someone that they are thinking of them.

Flowers are among the most remarkable structures in nature that bring glory to God. They are when nature wears a crown of glittering, functional colour that our Creator designed. Have you ever slowed down your life and studied the formation of a flower? The leaves, and then a flower bud miraculously appears, which grows and blooms into a spectacular declaration of colour that spans the spectrum, shape, texture, beauty and fills the air with divine perfumes that fill us with wonder and awe. This is God's romance. God's love. Flowers for us as a reminder.

"For ever since the world was created, people have seen the earth and sky. Through everything God made, they can clearly see his invisible qualities—his eternal power and divine nature. So they have no excuse for not knowing God." - Romans 1:20

You
Lisa K. Champion
Ménière's diagnosed in 2007
Photography

I've always said that sunsets were made by
God's paintbrush.

One evening I went down to Lake Michigan
and He had used some beautiful colors.

I never had Photoshop but with colors like this
who needs it!

So thankful that my Photography hobby lets me share
God's beautiful world around me.

Let Your Light Shine
G. Lakin Rosier II (VeDA Ambassador)
Pencil on paper

Matthew 5:15-16

15. Neither do men light a candle, and put it under a bushel, but on a candlestick; and it giveth light unto all that are in the house. 16. Let your light so shine before men, that they may see your good works, and glorify your Father which is in heaven.

One Sunday in church I was not feeling well, and wanted something to focus on to take my mind off my building Ménière's symptoms and to keep me awake. The speaker was talking about sharing the gospel and referenced *Matthew 5:15-16*. I started drawing a bushel basket with someone lifting it off of a candle. I used my hand as the model to remind myself to let my faith shine so others may see. In this day and age, it can be tempting to hide our faith for fear of being mocked and ridiculed, but when Jesus spoke these words, it was no easier for the followers of Christ to show their faith.

It took me several tries over several days before I was satisfied with the drawing. The basket was especially difficult.

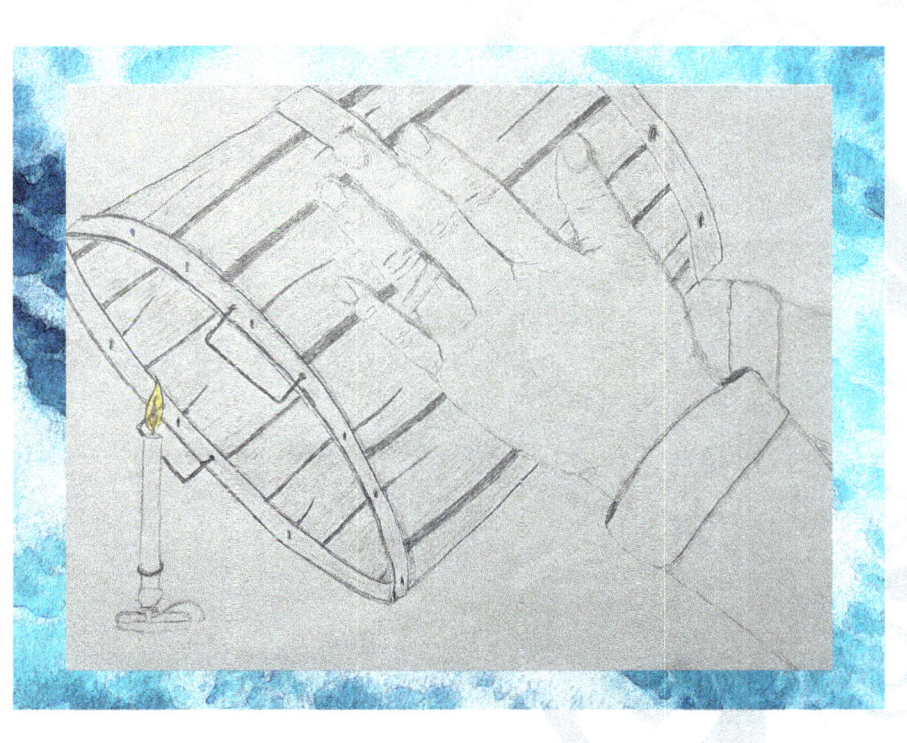

The Heavens Declare the Glory of God

Julieann Wallace, 2025
Acrylic Paint on Canvas
81.5cm x 61cm

Are you an opacarophile? A person who loves watching sunsets.

The Heavens Declare the Glory of God explores the vast colour spectrum of sunsets, and God's visually arresting canvas that evokes awe and wonder, slowing down time, making you feel good, reminding you that He is the creator of the heavens and earth.

"For ever since the world was created, people have seen the earth and sky. Through everything God made, they can clearly see his invisible qualities—his eternal power and divine nature. So they have no excuse for not knowing God." — Romans 1:20

He Lives
G. Lakin Rosier II (VeDA Ambassador)
Pencil on paper

On Easter a few years ago the theme was John 14:19: *Yet a little while, and the world me no more; but ye see me: because I live, ye shall live also.*

The hymn that followed was *Because*.
The following lines from the song stuck in my head the rest of the day. Especially the last line. The lesson and the hymn inspired me to draw the empty tomb with the caption, "He Lives".

BECAUSE
Because He walked the path, I know the way.
Because He calmed the storm, I'm not afraid.
Because He died for me, I'll live again.
Because He is my Friend, I'll follow Him.
Because He fills the world with light,
I'm filled with hope and peace.
And when He comes to earth again,
I'll kneel before His feet.
Because He gave to me ev'rything
He had to give,
I breathe, I see, I hope, I love, I live.

He Knows the Stars by Name
Julieann Wallace
Acrylic Paint on Canvas
12.7cm x 12.7cm

Psalm 19:1
To the choirmaster. A Psalm of David. The heavens declare the glory of God, and the sky above proclaims his handiwork.

Psalm 8:3-4
When I look at your heavens, the work of your fingers, the moon and the stars, which you have set in place, what is man that you are mindful of him, and the son of man that you care for him?

Psalm 147:4
He determines the number of the stars; he gives to all of them their names.

The Silver Lining
Lisa K. Champion
Photography

My world felt flooded when my hearing loss made me put my guitar down. But the silver lining was when I picked up a camera and started to see the beauty of the world around me. I started exploring the whole world of photography and it opened my eyes wider than they ever could see before. And all of this was an escape from my Ménière's disease and my other illnesses.

A few years ago, our street had flooded and even the news came to do a story about it. One day I was out with my camera after the water had gone down a bit and saw this silver lining - the ducks and the deer were just hanging out at the end of the street. Almost like a beautiful rainbow after the storm.

Lighthouse of the Lord
G. Lakin Rosier II (VeDA Ambassador)
Color pencil on paper

John 8:12: *Then spake Jesus again unto them, saying, I am the light of the world: he that followeth me shall not walk in darkness, but shall have the light of life.*

Lighthouses are often used as a metaphor for Jesus Christ. I was inspired to draw a lighthouse when Thomas S. Monson said, "My counsel for all of us is to look to the lighthouse of the Lord. There is no fog so dense, no night so dark, no gale so strong, no mariner so lost but what its beacon light can rescue. It beckons through the storms of life. The lighthouse of the Lord sends forth signals readily recognized and never failing."

I would add, following the light of Jesus can help us through the dark times caused by this dreadful disease.

Phi

Julieann Wallace
Acrylic on Canvas, Perspex overlay with paint pen
60cm x 40cm

Ocean waves rising and curling. Crashing. Calming. Relaxing. Running toward you but never reaching.
Jeremiah 5:22 '… I made the sand a boundary for the sea, an everlasting barrier it cannot cross. The waves may roll, but they cannot prevail; they may roar, but they cannot cross it.'
And so we sit on the beach, safe, and watch the waves curl in their Golden Ratio pattern. A spiral pattern that is a cosmic constant that governs the entire universe. The Creator's mark throughout all of His creation, plain for all of us to see.
His mark is in the ocean, plants, animals, flowers, cyclones, hurricanes, the human body, DNA and so on. God's mathematical pattern 1.618, represented by the Greek letter 'phi' (God loves maths!), a Creator who appears to delight in uniting form and function into the same structure.
The work of God's hands.

Romans 1:19-20
19 For what may be known about God is plain to them, because God has made it plain to them. 20 For since the creation of the world God's invisible qualities, His eternal power and divine nature, have been clearly seen, being understood from His workmanship, so that men are without excuse.

More Precious Than Gold, 2024
Julieann Wallace
Acrylic on Canvas
(57.5cm x 52.5cm)

1 Peter 1:7 *Your faith is more precious than gold.*
'More Precious Than Gold' consists of five pieces, each with the element of gold in different measures. The gold paint represents faith, a gift from God, which each of us has been given in different measures. It's important to remember that no one should consider themselves as superior to any other person with their measure of faith, but should instead recognize that God has placed them just where He wants them. And that is enough. Don't compare yourself to another.
Ephesians 2:8 *Faith is a gift from God. It is the first gift that is given to us.*
Equally, you may see the representation of faith in this art piece, about how you feel about your faith at times—ebbing and flowing like a stream, strong or sometimes weak. Perhaps your faith is tired, tested and torn. Trials and tribulations. Walk by faith and not by sight. It means choosing to wait on God's timing, even when it doesn't always make sense to us. But God's timing is always perfect.

1 Corinthians 13:13
Three things will last forever—faith, hope, and love— and the greatest of these is love.

Armor of God

G. Lakin Rosier II (VeDA Ambassador)
Pencil on paper

I created this drawing, pencil on paper, because I was inspired by *Ephesians 6:10-20*. It reminds me that if I go through life with the "Armor of God" as described in this scripture, I will be protected from the powers of the adversary.

Ephesians 6:10-20

10. Finally, my brethren, be strong in the Lord, and in the power of his might.
11 Put on the whole armour of God, that ye may be able to stand against the wiles of the devil.
12 For we wrestle not against flesh and blood, but against principalities, against powers, against the rulers of the darkness of this world, against spiritual wickedness in high places.
13 Wherefore take unto you the whole armour of God, that ye may be able to withstand in the evil day, and having done all, to stand.
14 Stand therefore, having your loins girt about with truth, and having on the breastplate of righteousness;
15 And your feet shod with the preparation of the gospel of peace;
16 Above all, taking the shield of faith, wherewith ye shall be able to quench all the fiery darts of the wicked.
17 And take the helmet of salvation, and the sword of the Spirit, which is the word of God:
18 Praying always with all prayer and supplication in the Spirit, and watching thereunto with all perseverance and supplication for all saints;
19 And for me, that utterance may be given unto me, that I may open my mouth boldly, to make known the mystery of the gospel,
20 For which I am an ambassador in bonds: that therein I may speak boldly, as I ought to speak.

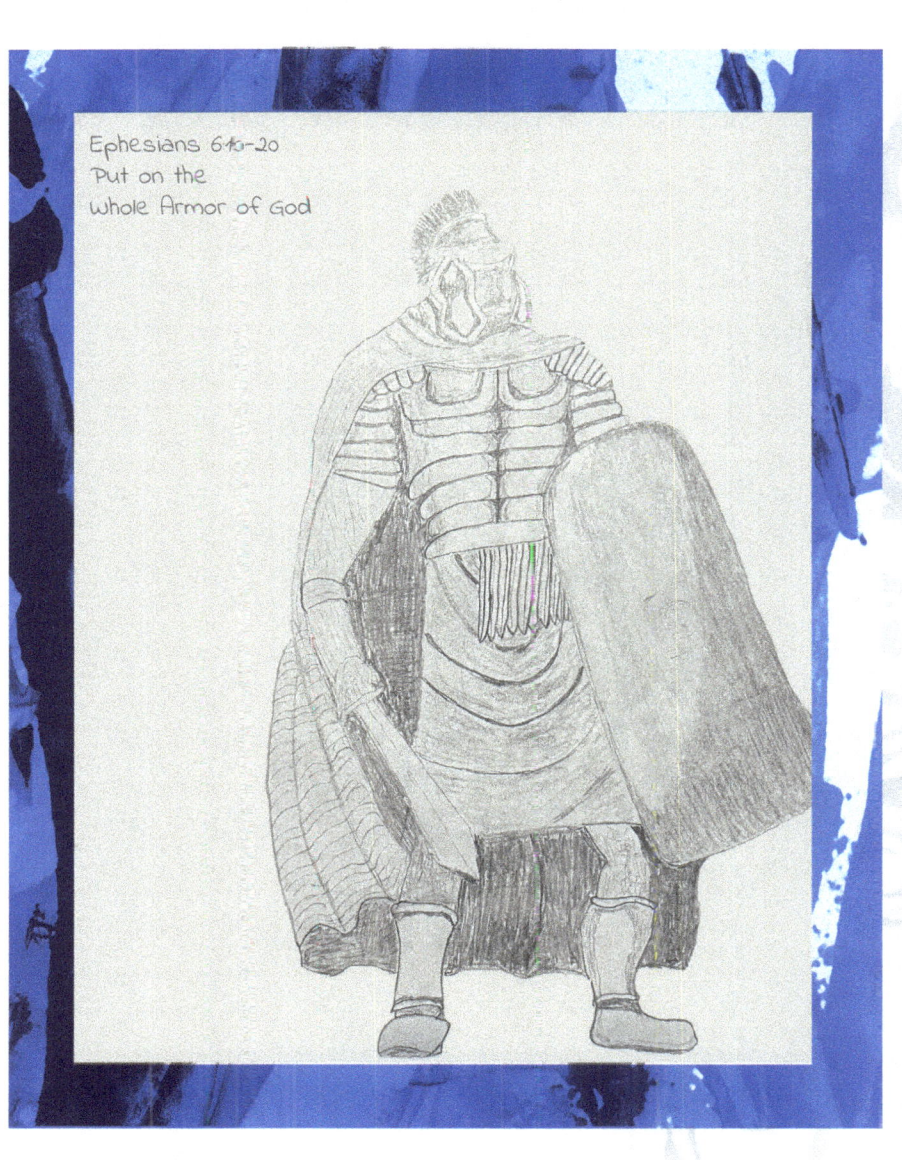

Blessed
Julieann Wallace
Acrylic Paint on Canvas
12.7cm x 12.7cm x 4cm

Isaiah 41:10
Fear not, for I am with you; be not dismayed, for I am your God; I will strengthen you, I will help you, I will uphold you with my righteous right hand.

James 1:12
Blessed is the person who remains steadfast under trial, for when they have stood the test they will receive the crown of life, which God has promised to those who love him.

Light at the End of the Tunnel
G. Lakin Rosier II (VeDA Ambassador)
Color pencil on paper

When my Ménière's disease symptoms became really bad, I became depressed. There did not seem to be a light at the end of the proverbial tunnel. My wife suggested I listen to a talk given by *Jeffrey R. Holland* and draw my impressions. This is the part that inspired me:

"There really is light at the end of the tunnel. It is the Light of the World, the Bright and Morning Star, the Light that is endless, that can never be darkened. It is the very Son of God Himself."

Listening to the talk, and thinking about it as I spent hours drawing it, made me remember there is hope. It helped to strengthen my faith in Jesus Christ.

Captive Art Series

Julieann Wallace, 2019
Mixed media – original watercolour and digital art using Procreate in iPad, combined and digitally printed before additional watercolour flowers added.

Captive art series - 4 Artworks
Size: 420mm x 297mm

1. *Once Upon a Time …*
2. *Until the Storm …*
3. *Hope …*
4. *Cured.*

The *Captive Art Series* consists of four artworks representing the turbulent journey of diagnosis of Ménière's disease. Life before, life during, hope never-ending, and looking to the future for a cure. Colour and symbolism are subtly imbued in each of the pieces to evoke and connect to emotions of each stage of the journey, with vertigo roses linking the four artworks.

Dedicated to those who live with Ménière's disease.
A cure will be found.

(Ménière's Awareness Advocate and philanthropist,
Ménière's Research Australia Ambassador,
Cochlear Implant Buddy)

Once upon a time...

The artwork depicts the pale colours of undervalue, representing taking your health, life, and the world around you as a given, while freely flying to reach your dreams and aspirations. *The colour of freedom.* God's light is small as His presence is taken for granted.

Once upon a time...

life was good. The colour of freedom. Dreaming dreams. Love. Wishes. Happy Friends. No fear. Unstoppable. Family. Twinkling stars. Flying free in body and mind. Dreams to live. So many pathways. The world is calling. Contented. Joy. Peace. Celebrate. Passions. Laughter. A beautiful life. Life without a care. Sport. Success. Unlimited food choices. Dance. No limits. Optimism. Sunrises. Sunsets. Life passes by in faded colours... did you even notice the small things?

until the Storm...

The colour of broken - dark volatile colours, with swirls for the unknown of vertigo, depression, and an unforeseeable, unpredictable future. The once fully yellow bird is losing its colour. The world around it has lost its appeal as the heaviness of Ménière's disease takes hold. The birdsong has lost its bass, as it loses the lower sounds of hearing from Ménière's disease.

Yet, the presence of God, represented by the light, is shining brighter, reminding us that God is always near.

until the **Storm**...

of incurable disease. The colour of broken. Anger. Depression. Frustration. Loss of self. Why? I want me back! Debilitating. Loneliness. Imprisoned inside a disabled body. My world is spinning. Violently. Stop! Hearing loss. Tinnitus so loud it's driving me insane. Faith. Please. Fight. Never give up. Never. So dark inside. Fear. Existing, but not living. I'm so, so tired. Broken dreams. Life. Courage. Vertigo. I hate you... I HATE YOU!! Captive. Breathe...

Hope...

The colour of belief. Hope in God that good things are coming. Yet, the bird's colour is pale and its wings are clipped, rendering it captive, unable to fly free from the condition, limiting life quality. The birdsong is still only in treble, as Ménière's has taken the hearing from one of the bird's ears. It is the hope and belief in God that lifts the spirit of the bird. God is always with us.

Hope...

Yet, there is hope. The colour of belief. Good things are coming. Hope for a cure. All things are possible. Patience. Notice the small things. Don't judge. I will find me in my messy, chaotic, difficult life. Capture moments. Be kind. Be gentle. Forgive. Thankfulness.

Freed.

The colour of happy. An imaginable colour of gratitude. An explosion of bright colours in all the elements showing happiness and thankfulness to God.

The fully restored bird, including return of hearing, represents God's healing, whether by His hand or by medical treatments and hearing technology, human intelligence gifted to us by God.

The bird is dropping a swirl of vertigo, never to be seen or felt again, while the light represents God's extravagant love, always remembered by the bird, and being the wind beneath the bird's wings.

Freed. ♡

Beyond thankful. Embrace life, it's a gift. The colour of happy. Love with all my heart. Fearless. Never forget my journey.

Aurora Borealis
From just outside of Umeå, Sweden
Tåsjön (Toe Lake), Sweden
Photo credits: *Camilla Konradsson*

Camilla is a photographer and artist who lives in Northern Sweden near the Artic Circle. Her photos are used here, with her permission, to show the beauty of God's work, and the talent the Lord gave her.

The beauty of nature always reminds me that Jesus is the ultimate artist, and any art we create is just a poor imitation of his work. It also reminds me of the parable of the talents in Matthew 25: 15-29:

15 And unto one he gave five talents, to another two, and to another one; to every man according to his several ability; and straightway took his journey.

In biblical times a talent was about 20 years of wages for a laborer. Being a parable, I like the analogy that it referred the God given talents we each receive. In the parable, two of those who received the talents increased the value. One buried his talent and did not increase its value, so it was taken away.

This parable has inspired me to increase my talents, admire the talents of others, and ultimately the talents of the Creator of all things.

G. Lakin Rosier II

Dear Lord,

Here I am with pen and paper, in our sacred garden where we talk. Just You and me, surrounded by Your flowers, breathtaking and fragrant. You, accepting me.
Just as I am. And I'm so thankful.

I'm overcome.

I'm bursting with overwhelming emotion and my tears want to fall. I have no words as I inhale that sacred breath You gift me. It's just… *it's just too much…*

I exhale.

I have no eloquent, silver-tongued words like a scholar to offer You, to write and to read to You with a whisper of deep love on the breeze.

It's just me, Lord. With a God-shaped heart and a profound adoration for You.

It's the work of Your hands, Lord, that gets me.
Your fingerprints. Over all of creation.
Over the heavens and the earth. *Over me.*

And I'm undone.

I'm overcome, Lord.

You see my tears and bottle them.
You see my struggle, my brokenness, my heart-wrenching moments... My helplessness. My rejection. My despair.

My worship in the unbearable storm.

I cry.

I wipe away my tear.

I have no controlled breath like a glassmith to offer You, creating lachrymatory bottles of every shape and size and colour to catch tears of grief, sealing them with Your knowing and understanding and love and compassion.

It's just me, with a broken hallelujah. Who depends on You with every breath I take.

It's my walk in life with You, Lord, knowing that I'm never alone that gets me. It's Your patience, Your compassion, Your tender concern for me, and the hope You give that lifts me.

Your healing.

Thank You for shining Your Light in the darkness.
Thank You for healing my brokenness.
Thank You for holding my hand. *Always.*

I exalt Thee.

And I'm overwhelmed, Lord.

And it's because of Your indescribable gift. *Jesus*.

I inhale deeply. I have no gift to bring that's fit for a King. No gold, frankincense or myrrh like the Magi to offer You, Lord, not even a drum.

It's just me. With a heart for Jesus.

My throat tightens.

His life. His human body. His human heart. His human mind. His human wills—one divine, one human. Without sin.

His marvellous, wonderful love.

I cry.

It's that You sent Your son, Lord, that gets me.
The perfect imprint of Your essence. Revealing You to me, and Your deep love for humanity.

And the love of Jesus, Lord... His compassion. His healing. His calling me by name.

Jesus is more than I ever deserve, God.
He walked upon the earth, for us, Lord. Undeserving us.

And this... He is a King, serving, instead of being served.

Unimaginable.

I'm overcome.

And it's because of You, Lord, and Your pursuit of me.
You strengthen me. You renew me. You lift me when I fall.

I bow my head.

I have no physical gift like an athlete to offer You, to run a race with agility and speed and strength, leaving a blazing, golden trail of acknowledgement of You before the crowd.

It's just me. Who bows down to You, straightening my imperishable crown of Life, that tilts and wobbles as I stumble, collecting Your glimmers and love and hope and encouragement on my fingertips on my life journey.

I couldn't do this without You.

It's Your presence, Lord, that gets me.
It's Your forgiveness. Your guidance. Your love for me.

And Your *Holy Spirit*.
There are no words... I'm beyond thankful.

And this. Our undeserved favour. *Grace.*

Never earned, but freely given. Thank You is never enough.

Please accept my eternal love for You, Lord, with all my heart and with all my soul and with all my mind and with all my strength.

Oh, Lord.

Prayer

Philippians 4:6-7

*Do not be anxious about anything,
but in everything by prayer and supplication with
thanksgiving, let your requests be made known to God.
And the peace of God, which surpasses all understanding,
will guard your hearts and your minds in Christ Jesus.*

Jeremiah 29:12-13

*Then you will call upon me and come and pray to me,
and I will hear you. You will seek me and find me when
you seek me with all your heart.*

Colossians 4:2

*Continue steadfastly in prayer,
being watchful in it with thanksgiving.*

1 Thessalonians 5:16-18

*Rejoice always, pray without ceasing,
give thanks in all circumstances;
for this is the will of God in Christ Jesus for you.*

Prayer

There are more than a million words in the English language according to a global language monitoring website. Yet, at times when we want to say a prayer to our Heavenly Father, we are at a loss for words. It's okay, God is not impressed by your word count.

And don't worry, *our mess of tangled emotions and scattered thoughts are completely known to God before we can so much as vocalize them - Zach Barnhart.*

And when we don't have the words, Jesus speaks to the Father on our behalf (Romans 8:34), in the same way the Holy Spirit helps us in our weakness. *We do not know what we ought to pray for, but the Spirit himself intercedes for us through wordless groans* (Romans 8:26)

Prayer is just like a conversation with him. There is no right or wrong way to pray. The Lord is just thrilled to hear from you.

You can pray from your heart aloud, or silently in a quiet place.

And if you'd like some extra help, we have added some prayers for you.

A prayer written for us by *Darlene Zschech*, an Australian Pentecostal Christian worship leader, singer, pastor, and author, who has written more than 80 published worship songs, and 6 books. You may know her worship song, 'Shout to the Lord'. She is described as a pioneer of the modern global worship movement. She is the lead pastor of *Hope Unlimited Church*, Australia, with her husband, *Mark Zschech*. Thank you, Darlene, for writing a prayer for us. We are so thankful. xx

My Dear Jesus,

Today I come to You with a beyond grateful heart. Even though I have sensed Your nearness for most of my life, during this last season of drawn out despair, the reality of the peace of Your presence has become my defining hope. Thankyou for seeing me, thankyou for hearing me, thankyou for Your faithful love and wrap around presence that literally holds me through every storm.

To try to put the wonder of your kindness in this simple prayer almost eludes me, yet I sense the beautiful invitation from Your heart to mine, to come before You with heartfelt worship, to pray, to sing, to respond with an authentic cry of gratitude and joy. I love that You never ask for eloquence or performance, but You love that I continue to come in childlike faith as I express my heart to You.

Psalm 100... I know this to be true.
4 Enter his gates with thanksgiving,
    and his courts with praise!
    Give thanks to him; bless his name!
5 For the Lord is good;
    his steadfast love endures forever,
    and his faithfulness to all generations.

Your goodness is beyond comparison, and while I continue to learn to TRUST You completely, Your patience is never exhausted while You wait with me. And so I will continue to praise Your name with every breath I have.

You are and will always be my confident Hope.

You are the testament of my life.

You are the Only One who gives us the oil of joy for mourning, the garment of praise instead of a spirit of heaviness.

All my trust is in You Jesus, the glory and the lifter of my head.

Amen

Heavenly Father,

Thank you for my life, and that I am so privileged to bear witness to the work of Your hands.

I come before You today, Father, with a body burdened by illness. You are the great healer, and I place my trust in Your loving hands.

Grant me strength to endure this trial and courage to face each day.

Pour out Your healing grace upon my body, mind, and spirit. And if healing is not according to Your will, equip me and my loved ones with strength, clarity, and discernment.

And I pray that You will grant me Your peace, which surpasses all understanding, to fill my hearts as I endure the days of my Ménière's disease.

In the midst of my weakness, be my strength. I surrender myself to Your care, trusting that Your love will sustain me.

In Jesus' name I pray,
Amen

A prayer written by *Rebecca Barlow Jordan*. Used with permission. Rebecca Barlow Jordan is a day-voted follower of Jesus with a passion for helping others find joy and purposeful living through deeper intimacy with God. As a bestselling, inspirational author, she has authored, co-authored, and contributed to over 30 books. Thank you, Rebecca. Be blessed.

A Prayer for Personal Healing

God, You know me so well. You created me. You know the number of hairs on my head, and You even know the thoughts conceived in my heart before I ever vocalize them. You've told us to come to You and ask for every need of life. You are Jehovah-Rapha, the God who heals, and You have the final word on my destiny, the number of years I'll live and serve You on earth.

I'm coming to You today as Your child, longing to hear from You and asking for Your divine healing. There's so much I don't understand about life. But I do know that with one touch, one word, You can make me whole. Please forgive me of my sins, cleanse me of my unrighteousness, and begin Your healing from the inside out.

I don't always know what Your will is Lord, especially in times like now, when I desperately seek Your face. I'm offering You no promises, no bargains, no deals to exchange for my health. I simply bow my heart before You to tell You the desire of my heart: that I want to spend as many years as I can loving You here, loving others, and wanting to become more like You. However You choose to accomplish that is up to You—and okay with me. If You use doctors to provide healing, give them wisdom to know what to do.

Regardless of how You accomplish it, the healing You give is always miraculous. And You deserve all the praise.

I absolutely believe You have the power to heal. You demonstrated that on earth, and You still heal in miraculous ways today. Even when my faith is weak, You say it is enough, and my love for You is strong. And I know You already hold my heart and life in Your hands. It's up to You. If I can bring You more glory through healing, then that's what I ask for. That's what I desire.

But if Your answer is no, or not now, I know that Your grace is sufficient for me. Ultimately, I want Your will to be my will. I look forward to spending an eternity with You.

But Lord, if You have planned still more for me to do here on this earth, I not only need and want Your physical healing, Lord, but a thorough, deep-down cleansing and strengthening—a wholehearted renewal of all that I am. Because all that I am is Yours. Use this trial to strengthen me from a "what-if" faith to a "no-matter-what" faith. And no matter what, I choose to honor You and give You glory.

In Jesus's name, Amen.
© 2015, Rebecca Barlow Jordan

Heavenly Father,

Help me to keep my focus on You
when my symptoms are overwhelming.

Help me be faithful and see the good and blessings
surrounding me.

Please strengthen my mind, heart, and body, and
heal me today.

May the Holy Spirit guide me in peace and comfort.

In Jesus' name, Amen.

Heavenly Father,

I come to You in the name of Jesus. Your Word says, "Whosoever shall call on the name of the Lord shall be saved" (Acts 2:21).

I am calling on You. I pray and ask Jesus to come into my heart and be Lord over my life according to Romans 10:9-10. "If thou shalt confess with thy mouth the Lord Jesus, and shalt believe in thine heart that God hath raised him from the dead, thou shalt be saved."

I do that now. I confess that Jesus is Lord, and I believe in my heart that God raised Him from the dead.

Thank You for giving me the gift of eternal life.

I pray this in the name of Jesus,
Amen

Serenity Prayer

God, grant me the serenity
To accept the things I cannot change;
Courage to change the things I can;
And wisdom to know the difference.

Living one day at a time;
Enjoying one moment at a time;
Accepting hardships as the pathway to peace;
Taking, as He did, this sinful world
As it is, not as I would have it;

Trusting that He will make all things right
If I surrender to His Will;
So that I may be reasonably happy in this life
And supremely happy with Him Forever and ever in the next.

Amen

Dear Lord,

I am overwhelmed and humbled that I can come before You and speak to You. Not only do I communicate with You, but You always listen and guide me on the right path.

Thank You for always being there for me, whether I realize it or not. Your love washes over me daily, hourly, and moment-by-moment. I am so fortunate to have You walking with me and loving me, for Your goodness knows no bounds. I am overwhelmed with Your goodness and love for me, and for the unceasing love You have shown me throughout my life.

You've loved me when I haven't deserved it.

I am so thankful that You accept my prayers and despite all of my failings, You still look upon me with love with joy and acceptance.

Thank You for being so good to me.
Thank You for who You are!

You truly are an amazing God!

In Jesus' name I pray,
Amen

Heavenly Father,

Thank You for the days I got out of bed, even though it was a struggle through the vertigo, the dizziness, the brain fog, the fatigue, the migraine, the tinnitus, the nausea, the lack of balance, the sensitivities to sound and light. I know it was You who helped me.

Thank You for helping me to help others, even when I was pouring from my empty jug. I know it was You who helped me, and will refill my jug. Please bless those I helped.

Thank You for moments of joy when I least expected it, lifting me to a place of praise and gratitude. You know exactly what I need, even when I don't.

Thank You Lord. Thank You for everything You have done for me, and will do for me.

And I know Lord, that day is coming when I will be free from my physical symptoms. Released. And made new. I look forward to that day, surrounded by Your Love and Light and Your words to welcome me home.

My eternal thanks to You, Lord. I am Yours, and You are mine.

In Jesus' name I pray, Amen.

Heavenly Father,

I praise You for You are good, and are with me always in the storm, even when I can't feel Your presence. Thank You for this day, Lord, and thank You for hearing my prayer, that You hear my words and see my heart and my hurt. You know me by name, Lord, You formed in the womb, and You see my tears and bottle them.

I ask You, Lord, for Your healing, physically, spiritually, emotionally, because I know that all things are possible with You. I also know, Lord, that healing takes time, and that You will give me God whispers while I wait patiently, to lift my heart and spirit.

Thank You Lord, for my family and friends. I ask You to bless them as they care for me and give me support as I navigate my way back to wellness.

Heavenly Father, I place myself into Your hands so You can carry me through this difficult time, and I'll look for your God glitters, Your gifts to focus on, to give me moments of joy and lift me, and to know Your peace. I love You, Lord.

I ask for these things, trusting in Your timing.

In the name of Jesus, Amen.

*To touch Your robe is all I need, Jesus.
Thank you, God, for your Indescribable gift.*

Morning Prayer

Dear Lord,

What a blessed morning it is. Thank You for allowing me to take another breath today. Before my feet touch the floor I open my heart to You.

As I rise today, steady my breath, my steps and my mind. Calm any fear, overwhelm or negative thinking, and fill that space with Your everlasting peace.

Remind me to breathe deeply when life's stressors or vestibular symptoms surface. With each intentional, slow inhale, allow my anxiety to soften. With each slow exhale, let a calmness wash over me, the calm that only Your presence can offer.

Remind me in these moments that I am not alone on this journey, that Your presence embodies a bubble of strength surrounding me. Guide me to notice the God winks and glimmers throughout the day, especially during challenging moments.

Surround me with kindness, compassion and understanding and help me to offer those same gifts to others that cross my path.

Lord, as I go out into the world please cover me in Your grace. Let Your mercy revitalize my hope, Your love steady my steps, and Your faithfulness carry me steadily through whatever the day holds.

In Jesus' name, Amen.

Everlasting Father,

I pray today that You come down and be with every person that is struggling with vestibular disease - with the dizziness, the fear, the doubt, and the exhaustion - affecting every aspect of their everyday lives.

I know You are the same God of Daniel, Job, and Paul.

I know that You provided hope, encouragement and deliverance for them then, and I have full faith that You are the hope and encouragement and deliverance for us today.

I pray for relief, strength, and peace.

I pray that they will feel Your presence, Your power and the hope and the love that comes with You.

I ask in Your mighty name,
Amen.

Heavenly Father,

We ask for Your healing touch on my wife's body, relieving her dizziness and imbalance.

Grant her peace and strength to navigate each day, and give us both wisdom and patience as we face this challenge together.

In Jesus' name,
Amen.

Dear God,

    Yeah, it's me again. My usual prayers are full of cuss words and diatribes about how I need You to fix certain things. I know You never fail me, but again, I like the fact You take us as we are: here and now in OUR present situations. But this is different. I'm praying for a community. And I hope You're listening. We, the silent sufferers, need a rock to stand on. I believe You too be that rock. Give us peace on this earth You created. Give us patience as we navigate our disease, our relationships, and our heart that yearns for You and Your comfort.

    May Your will be done on earth as it is in heaven, full restoration and reconciliation of all things so that we can have that hope. Give me the grace to let each person be themselves under whatever circumstances they find themselves in. But even more, help me to find the grace I need to carry on in my battles. Heaven and Hell are on earth right here, right now. Unveil Your presence to me so that I may not grow weary. Help me fight the good fight, You know I can't do it alone. Thank You for this miraculous life you've given me. Thank You for allowing me the privilege to carry my burdens with humility and grace in the face of tremendous odds. I'm one of the lucky ones! Please take care of us!

    Peace out my Father, my Tutor, my Bro, my Mentor, my Safe Landing, my Infinite Creator. Love from you're not so humble, stumbling in the dark, confused but not defeated servant.

Steve Schwier

The Lord's Prayer

The Lord's Prayer the Lord Jesus taught His disciples in Matthew 6:9-13 and Luke 11:2-4. Matthew 6:9-13

Our Father, who is in heaven,
hallowed be your name.
thy kingdom come,
thy will be done,
on earth as it is in heaven.
give us this day our daily bread,
and forgive us our trespasses,
as we forgive those who trespass against us.
And lead us not into temptation,
but deliver us from evil.
For thine is the kingdom,
the power and the glory
for ever and ever.

Amen.

Acknowledgements

First and always, God. Thank You for everything You do for us, especially when we cannot see it, or feel it. Your grace is sufficient. *Always.* There are no words for the endless praise and thankfulness we feel.

Thankful. Grateful. Blessed.

A *huge* thank you to *Heather Davies, Angela Selar, Kim M. Rosier, Steven Schwier, G. Lakin Rosier,* and *Dave Giugno* for their support when I put out a call to help me create this book. Your help and friendship mean the world to me, not just now, but for the *v-e-r-y* long time that we have known each other in Ménière's disease Facebook groups - *Julieann* x

Behind In the Storm - *His Love*

Julieann Wallace

Julieann Wallace kept hearing a call to create a book of faith for people with Ménière's disease in church, numerous times in 2024 and 2025. She decided to act on it, and gathered a team around her of people with Ménière's that she knew loved the Lord, and is forever thankful for their support. It was *Angela Selar* who suggested we broaden the book to include other Vestibular conditions as well.

Julieann is proud to be a voice for those whose lives have been changed by vestibular disorders, her creativity in writing and art, playing a significant role in her story of overcoming Ménière's, and of illuminating others experiencing the tumultuous journey of vertigo, tinnitus and hearing loss.

Julieann was diagnosed with Ménière's in 1995. In 2002, after a particular vicious vertigo attack, she vowed to help find a cure for Ménière's however that looked, thinking it would be just trialling medications. She never saw books or art as part of her plan.

In 2004, she chose to have the full strength ototoxic Gentamicin injected into her left ear, knowing she would be sacrificing her balance and hearing. She wanted her life back. She wanted to be able to enjoy raising her three children. And she has been vertigo free since and returned to teaching. It was an answered prayer.

In 2013, she wrote a children's picture book called 'Vanilla Swirl', for kids with a mum with Ménière's. It sold well, and profits were donated to Ménière's Research in Australia. She then wrote 'Blueberry Swirl' for Dads with Ménière's.

After two of her MD friends took their lives, Julieann set about making the invisible Ménière's disease, visible. By the grace of God, she penned a bestselling novel with a Ménière's character with an unshakable faith, 'The Colour of Broken (2018)', twice longlisted to be made into a movie, and #1 on Amazon numerous times. The Audiobook was narrated by the amazing *Heather Davies*. Julieann wrote the sequel, 'All the Colours Above (2021)' (dedicating it to the late *Judy McNamara Tripp*, founder of *The Ménière's Awareness Project)*, due to reader requests, where she cures Ménière's with nanobot biomedicine technology. She is the author of the 'Daily Ménière's Journal', and 'It Will Change Your Life ~ a cochlear implant journey', and 'Ménière's Woman'.

In 2023, Julieann spearheaded 'Dear Ménière's – Letter & Art' (with *Heather Davies*, *Steven Schwier* and *Anne Elias*), putting out a global callout for people with Ménière's to submit letters and art. It was an Amazon #1 bestseller in its category.

In 2023, Julieann released a middle school chapter book called 'The Adventures of Captain Vertigo … and Fart Man' – a superhero with a cochlear implant, using his superpowers of Ménière's to fight crime. Humor is a key ingredient to help kids understand hearing loss and their parent with Ménière's disease.

In December, 2025, Julieann released a Ménière's Cookbook, 'Welcome to our Table - A Ménière's Low-Sodium Cookbook', the recipes collated from people living with Ménière's, and also, this book of faith.

She donates 100% of profits from the sales of her Ménière's books to research to help find a cure.

Julieann has also released 10 fiction novels under her pen name of *Amelia Grace* so far, and always mentions Ménière's disease in them somewhere.

Julieann is a *Ménière's Research Australia Ambassador*, *Cochlear Implant Buddy* with Cochlear Australia, and is also a part-time secondary teacher, artist, chocoholic, tea ninja, paper cut survivor, and tries not to scare off her cat, Claude Monet, or her dog, Pablo Picasso, with her terrible cello playing. In 2020, she received a cochlear implant, hearing again. An answered prayer.

Julieann is forever thankful to God for His unfailing love and grace and mercy, and answered prayers, and His gentle pursuit to continually remind her that she is a child of God.

www.julieannwallaceauthor.com

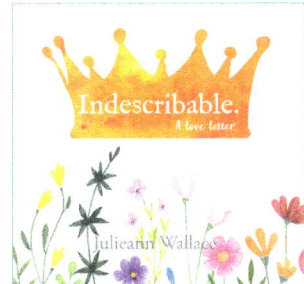

Angela Selar

Angela Selar's journey with vestibular symptoms began at birth, when she was born hard of hearing, and with vestibular issues.

When she was thirteen, she was diagnosed with bilateral Ménière's. Vestibular symptoms have constantly been a part of her life. Genetic factors come into play, as others in her family have been diagnosed with Ménière's disease.

She went on to obtain her Bachelor of Education, with a minor in Geology and Astronomy from the University of Toledo in 1993, and worked towards her Master's in Special Needs/Language Specialist and Deaf Education at Notre Dame College in Cleveland, Ohio.

Her advocacy for vestibular disorders began over a decade ago, drawing from her own journey as a lifelong bilateral Ménière's and vestibular patient.

For over seven years, she has been running online support groups, pouring into others walking a similar path with vestibular disorders, helping them move through life with their challenging symptoms.

Heather Davies

Heather Davies was diagnosed with Ménière's disease and Vestibular Migraine in 2017, soon after she became VeDA Ambassador to raise awareness for vestibular disorders.

She first shared her voice as narrator of 'The Color of Broken' on Audible, a beautifully written novel by *Julieann Wallace*, under her pen name, *Amelia Grace*, giving listeners a window into the world of Ménière's. Heather went on to create the *Ménière's Muse podcast*, where patients share their very personal stories living with vestibular disorders. These stories inspire hope, as well as bring connection to the vestibular community.

Her love for advocacy work shines through as a patient panel moderator for VeDA's Life Rebalanced Live Conference the last couple years, and most recently being invited to speak at the *2025 Ménière's Disease Symposium*, where she shared a patient's perspective of living with Ménière's disease. She believes in the power of connection, and encourages warriors to find strength by leaning on the vestibular community so that no one feels alone. Find her *Ménière's Muse Podcast* on Spotify, Apple, YouTube or anywhere you listen to your favorite podcasts!

Kim M. Rosier

Kim M. Rosier does not have Ménière's, but is the very supportive spouse of Lakin Rosier. She does suffer from her own chronic illnesses, such as diabetes, fibromyalgia, migraines generalized anxiety disorder, and depression. This allows Kim and Lakin to understand and sympathize with each other in their struggles.

Kim has held executive assistant positions in multiple industries, including; boat manufacturing, copy and publishing, county government, and facility operations of an NFL team. In those positions she wrote, proofread and edited communications on a daily basis. She is a valuable proofreader for this book.

Recently, Kim has been studying Italian on DuoLingo, but her favorite job ever is being a wife, a mother and especially a Nonna.

Steve Schwier

Steven Schwier was diagnosed with Ménière's in 2012. In the month of September, 2020, Steve rode an e-bike, 400 miles from Denver, Colorado to Columbus, Ohio to bring awareness to Ménière's disease.

His difficult and grueling ride is chronicled in his memoir, 'On the Vertigo: One Sick Man's Journey to Make a Difference'. His ride raised more than $10,000, all of which went to Ménière's disease awareness and research.

Steve is the founder of *On the Vertigo Org* - a nonprofit seeking to provide community and support to those with Ménière's disease, while raising awareness and funding research. He is also a VeDA Ambassador.

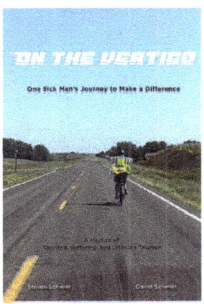

Dave Giugno

Dave Giugno has had Ménière's since 2014. He is known online as the Ménière's Disease Warrior with his YouTube channel, and is a *VeDA Ambassador*.

He has a vlog to talk about his journey and spread awareness of Ménière's as well as helping others deal with this disease. He co-founded two Ménière's support groups on Facebook - *Ménière's and Vertigo without Borders* and *Ménière's and Vertigo with Christian Borders*.

His warcry is to help people and let them know they are not alone, and stresses that with Ménière's, we all have the same disease but we are all different. What triggers one person may not trigger another. What works for one person may not work for another. Better days are coming.

Ménière's Disease Warrior!! - *YouTube*

G. Lakin Rosier II (Lakin)

G. Lakin Rosier II (Lakin) was bilateral when diagnosed with Ménière's in 2010, but had symptoms in the left ear for at least 30 years prior to that.

He also has vestibular migraines, although that diagnosis was fairly recent. When diagnosed, he became active in the Ménière's Facebook community. After going on Government disability in 2015, he was asked to moderate/admin several Facebook Ménière's pages.

In February of 2022, he helped to start the Ménière's Disease Zoom Support Group, and continues to co-host those meetings.

In November 2025, he was honored to become a *VeDA Ambassador*.

Helping people learn to manage their Ménière's symptoms, through the zoom group and Facebook pages, has given him the purpose in his life that was lost when he could no longer work.

Lakin finds joy in drawing and painting, which he never had time to try prior to being on disability. He has a very supportive wife, two understanding adult children, and in 2024, became a granddad, which he loves.

Thank you for reading our book.

It is our hope that you find a place
to connect, and to listen, and to pray
to God in the name of Jesus.

And to borrow the words from
Nigerian gospel singer Sinach's song, *Way Maker,*
Jesus is moving in our midst as a waymaker,
miracle worker, promise keeper, light in the darkness,
even when we don't see it, He never stops working.

It is our *prayer* that our Heavenly Father
and Lord and Saviour, Jesus,
bless you and keep you
and make his face shine upon you
and give you peace.

www.ingramcontent.com/pod-product-compliance
Lightning Source LLC
Chambersburg PA
CBHW061213070526
44583CB00025B/3229